Arthur Penrhyn Stanley

The Bible : Its Form and Its Substance

Three Sermons Preached Before the University of Oxford

Arthur Penrhyn Stanley

The Bible : Its Form and Its Substance
Three Sermons Preached Before the University of Oxford

ISBN/EAN: 9783337100278

Printed in Europe, USA, Canada, Australia, Japan

Cover: Foto ©Lupo / pixelio.de

More available books at **www.hansebooks.com**

THE BIBLE:
ITS FORM AND ITS SUBSTANCE.

Three Sermons

PREACHED BEFORE

THE UNIVERSITY OF OXFORD,

BY

ARTHUR PENRHYN STANLEY, D.D.,

REGIUS PROFESSOR OF ECCLESIASTICAL HISTORY,
AND CANON OF CHRIST CHURCH.

Oxford and London:
JOHN HENRY AND JAMES PARKER.
1863.

PREFACE.

THE three following Sermons were preached in consecutive order during the last two years before the University of Oxford. The substance of much of the first two has been printed already elsewhere—one in my Lectures on the Eastern Church, the other in my Lectures on the Jewish Church. It has occurred to me, however, that there might be some to whom the publication of them in their original connexion might be of use: the more so, as they are the direct expositions of a text which has long appeared to me to contain not merely the best definition which the Bible contains of its own structure and contents, but also to give the best reply to many of the difficulties which have of late years beset the path of the theological student.

Some years ago this noble passage was invested to me with an additional interest by an incident which befel me in Russia. I was on my way to the country residence of the venerable Archbishop and Metropolitan of Moscow, Philaret, in company with a Russian General, who had undertaken to act as interpreter. During our drive we discussed the topics of conversation suitable to the interview; and I suggested some question relating to the Old Testament, as a subject to which, it was understood, the Metropolitan had paid special attention. The General himself started the difficulty which, he said, had often occurred to him, of the apparent vindictiveness and cruelty of the precepts in the Old Testament, compared with the milder spirit of the New. We discussed this difficulty as we went; and I ventured, amongst other solutions, to suggest the words of the text, which, as well as the Epistle from which it is taken, was wholly new to him. In the interview with the Archbishop which followed, this topic of the difference between the Old and the New Dispensations was the one which he introduced to the aged Primate. The Metropolitan immediately broke into an animated argument, in the course of which the General turned round with unfeigned astonishment and delight, and said, " He " has quoted the very same passage to which you " referred in our conversation, and has pointed out " how in the expression ' sundry times and divers " ' manners' there is a complete acknowledgment " of the gradual and various modes of imperfect " Revelation before the full light of Christianity."

It is indeed an obvious statement and answer of the whole difficulty. I mention this simple incident, first because it shews how naturally it occurs to serious students of the Old Testament under circumstances the most widely different; and secondly, because it shews how a doctrine which in our own country is often regarded at the present day with extreme hostility and suspicion, was familiar and congenial to the mind of the most venerable authority of the most orthodox of European Churches.

The explanation and expansion of this grand passage will sufficiently appear in the following pages. But it may be well to say a few words in answer to an objection, which, being of a controversial and temporary kind, I forbore from noticing in the Sermons themselves. It may be said that the doctrine contained in the Sacred Text is inconsistent with that theory of a uniform and equal Inspiration of every word and letter of the Bible, which is at present regarded almost as an article of faith by many religious persons in this country. That such a divergence exists, I freely admit. The doctrine of the author of this great Epistle, and the facts of the Bible generally, are alike irreconcileable with this modern hypothesis [a]. Neither is the theory to which I allude contained in any of the formularies of the Church of England. In the only [b] instances in which the word "Inspiration" and its cognate

---

[a] I have called it modern as regards the history of Christendom. No doubt such a theory prevailed in regard to the Old Testament amongst the Rabbinical schools. In Christian Theology, it appears to have been first systematised in the *Formula Consensus Helvetica*, 1675.

[b] The Collect in the Communion Service, "Cleanse the "thoughts of our hearts by the *inspiration* of Thy Holy Spirit;" the Collect for the Fifth Sunday after Easter, "That by Thy "holy *inspiration* we may think those things that be good;" the Prayer for the Church Militant, "*Inspire* continually the "Universal Church;" the *Veni Creator*, "Come, Holy Ghost, "our souls *inspire* ;" the XIIIth Article, "Works done before "the *inspiration* of Christ's Spirit."

verb are used in the Liturgy and in the Articles, the sense is invariably that of the Divine influence suggesting all good thoughts and wise counsels to the hearts and minds of all men. To deny this wide signification of the word, and to restrict its meaning to any single exercise of the Divine operations, would be an offence against the letter if not the spirit of the Formularies, which ought not to be needlessly incurred.

But without entering at length into the pretensions of the Helvetic theory of Inspiration, I have thought it right to state its general relations to Christianity and to the Bible in words, which may have more weight from having been written before the rise of those personal feelings which have of late so much embittered the controversy on this subject:—

"It is very true that our position with respect to
" the Scriptures is not in all points the same as our
" fathers'. For sixteen hundred years nearly, while
" physical science, and history, and chronology, and
" criticism, were all in a state of torpor, the ques-
" tions which now present themselves to our minds
" could not from the nature of the case arise.
" When they did arise, they came forward into
" notice gradually: first the discoveries in as-
" tronomy excited uneasiness; then as men began
" to read more critically, differences in the several
" Scripture narratives of the same thing awakened
" attention; more lately, the greater knowledge
" which has been gained of history, and of lan-
" guage, and in all respects the more careful in-

"quiry to which all ancient records have been
"submitted, have brought other difficulties to light,
"and some sort of answer must be given to them.

"It has unfortunately happened that the diffi-
"culties of the Scripture have been generally treated
"as objections to the truth of Christianity; as such
"they have been pressed by adversaries, and as
"such Christian writers have replied to them.

"Yet what conceivable connexion is there be-
"tween the date of Cyrenius's government, or the
"question whether our Lord healed a blind man as
"He was going into Jericho or as He was leaving
"it; or whether Judas bought himself the field of
"blood, or it was bought by the high priests: what
"connexion can there be between such questions,
"and the truth of God's love to man in the Re-
"demption and of the Resurrection of our Lord?
"Do we give to any narrative in the world, to any
"statement, verbal or written, no other alternative
"than that it must be either infallible or unworthy
"of belief? Is not such an alternative so ex-
"travagant as to be a complete reductio ad ab-
"surdum? And yet such is the alternative which
"men seem generally to have admitted in consider-
"ing the Scripture narratives: if a single error
"can be discovered, it is supposed to be fatal to
"the credibility of the whole.

"This has arisen from an unwarranted interpre-
"tation of the word 'inspiration,' and by a still
"more unwarranted inference. An inspired work
"is supposed to mean a work to which God has
"communicated His own perfections; so that the
"slightest error or defect of any kind in it is

"inconceivable, and that which is other than per-
"fect in all points cannot be inspired. This is
"the unwarranted interpretation of the word 'in-
"'spiration.' But then follows the still more un-
"warranted inference,—'If all the Scripture is not
"'inspired, Christianity cannot be true;' an infer-
"ence which is absolutely entitled to no other con-
"sideration than what it may seem to derive from
"the number of those who have either openly or
"tacitly maintained it.

"Most truly do I believe the Scriptures to be
"inspired; the proofs of their inspiration rise con-
"tinually with the study of them. The Scriptural
"narratives are not only about divine things, but
"are themselves divinely framed and superintended.
"I cannot conceive my conviction of this truth
"being otherwise than sure. Yet I must acknow-
"ledge that the Scriptural narratives do not claim
"this inspiration for themselves; so that if I should
"be obliged to resign my belief in it, which seems
"to me impossible, I yet should have no right to
"tax the Scriptures with having advanced a pre-
"tension proved to be unfounded; their whole
"credibility as a most authentic history of the
"most important facts would remain untouched.

"So much for the unwarranted inference, that, if
"the Scripture histories are not inspired, the great
"facts of the Christian Revelation cannot be main-
"tained. But it is no less an unwarranted inter-
"pretation of the term 'inspiration,' to suppose
"that it is equivalent to a communication of the
"Divine perfections. Surely, many of our words
"and many of our actions are spoken and done by

"the inspiration of God's Spirit, without whom we
"can do nothing acceptable to God. Yet does the
"Holy Spirit so inspire us as to communicate to
"us His own perfections? Are our best words or
"works utterly free from error or from sin? All
"inspiration does not then destroy the human
"and fallible part in the nature which it inspires;
"it does not change man into God. . . . .

"Feeling what the Scriptures are, I would not
"give unnecessary pain to any one by an enumera-
"tion of those points in which the literal historical
"statement of an inspired writer has been vainly
"defended. Some instances will probably occur to
"most readers; others are perhaps not known, and
"never will be known to many, nor is it at all
"needful or desirable that they should know them.
"But if ever they are brought before them, let
"them not try to put them aside unfairly, from
"a fear that they will injure our faith. Let us not
"do evil that evil may be escaped from; and it is
"an evil, and the fruitful parent of evils innumer-
"able, to do violence to our understanding or to
"our reason in their own appointed fields; to
"maintain falsehood in their despite, and reject the
"truth which they sanction.

"And if it should happen, as in all probability it
"will, that we shall be called upon to correct in
"some respects our notions as to the Scriptures,
"and so far to hold views different from those of
"our fathers, we should consider that our fathers
"did not, and could not stand in our circum-
"stances; that the knowledge which may call upon
"us to relinquish some of their opinions, was

"a knowledge which they had not. Till this know-
"ledge comes to us, let us hold our fathers'
"opinions as they held them; but when it does
"come it will come by God's will, and to do His
"work: and that work will, assuredly, not be our
"separation from our fathers' faith; but if we fol-
"low God's guidance humbly and cheerfully, cling-
"ing to God the while in personal devotion and
"obedience, we may be made aware of what to
"them would have been an inexplicable difficulty,
"and which was, therefore, hidden from their know-
"ledge; and yet, 'through the grace of our Lord
"'Jesus Christ,' we believe that we shall be saved
"even as they."—*Arnold's Sermons,* vol. iv. pp. 485—492.

This is the statement of the case by one who was no doubt frequently assailed in his lifetime, although since his removal from amongst us no one has ventured to bring against him the charges of unbelief which are now for similar statements so freely employed against the living. But it may be well to shew that the same sentiments are substantially shared by those who have not encountered any serious obloquy for their opinions. I subjoin extracts from two volumes which have recently appeared, the one with the sanction of the present Bishop of Oxford, the other with the sanction and concurrence of the present Archbishop of York:—

"To declare that there are no interpolations or
"corruptions in the Sacred Volume is to make an
"assertion improbable *à priori,* and at variance

"with the actual phenomena. The sober-minded
" in every age have allowed that the written Word,
" as it has come down to us, has these slight im-
" perfections, which no more interfere with its value
" than the spots upon the sun detract from his
" brightness, or than a few marred and stunted
" forms destroy the harmony and beauty of Nature."
—*Aids to Faith*, p. 247.

" All such terms as 'mechanical' and 'dynamical'
" inspiration, and all the theories that have grown
" round these epithets—all such distinctions as in-
" spirations of superintendence, inspirations of sug-
" gestion, and so forth—all attempts again to draw
" lines of demarcation between the inspiration of
" the books of Scripture themselves and the inspi-
" ration of the authors of which those books were
" results—may be most profitably dismissed from
" our thoughts, and the whole subject calmly re-
" considered from what may be termed a Scriptural
" point of view. The holy Volume itself shall ex-
" plain to us the nature of that influence by which
" it is pervaded and quickened. Thus far we are
" perfectly in accord with our opponents. We are
" agreed on both sides that there *is* such a thing
" as inspiration in reference to the Scriptures, and
" we are further agreed that the Scriptures them-
" selves are the best sources of information on the
" subject."—*Aids to Faith*, p. 404.

" Origen was the first great Biblical critic: few
" things have tended more than Biblical criticism
" to modify the theory of verbal inspiration; and
" this appeared even in the patristic ages and among
" some of the most illustrious of the patristic writers.

"The critical labours of Chrysostom and Jerome, in the beginning of the fifth century, made them observe the apparent discrepancies in the accounts of the Evangelists, and other like difficulties in Holy Writ. Such observations led to a greater appreciation of the human element in the composition of Scripture. St. Chrysostom could see that some slight variations in the different narratives of the same event were no cause for anxiety or unbelief, but rather a proof that the Evangelists were independent witnesses. And St. Jerome could discern in the New Testament writers a dialect inferior to the purest Greek, and even at times a mixture of human passion in the language of the Apostles."—*Aids to Faith*, p. 290.

"Some Christian controversialists, who take high grounds themselves, write as if they thought that Christianity was not worth defending, unless it was defended exactly on their principles. The minds of the young, more especially, are sometimes greatly endangered by this means. The defender of the Gospel may be but an indifferent reasoner. He fails to make his ground sure and strong. His reader finds more forcible, at least more specious, arguments elsewhere. He thinks the advocate he rested on defeated, his arguments answered and upset, and Christianity itself seems lost. Now, we may surely begin by saying, that the question of inspiration is, within certain limits, a question *internal* to Christianity. No doubt it may materially affect the evidences of Christianity; but the questions of verbal inspiration, mechanical inspiration, dynamical inspiration, and the "like, are all questions on which persons believing in the Gospel may differ. There is a degree of latitude which must be fatal to faith; but within certain limits men may differ, and yet believe.

"We have a number of different books written in different styles, indicating the different characters of the writers. At times, too, there appear slight diversities of statements in trifling matters of detail. Here we mark a human element. If God spoke, it is plain that He spoke through man; if God inspired, He inspired man. Even the Gospel *miracles* were often worked with some instrumental means; no wonder, then, that when God would teach men, He would teach through human agency. And the difference of style— perhaps the slight discrepancies in statements— seem to satisfy us that some portions at least of the Bible were not simply dictated by God to man; there was not what is called mere mechanical or organic inspiration; God did not simply speak God's words, using as a mere machine man's lips to speak them with."—*Aids to Faith*, p. 302.

"There is no attaining a satisfactory view of the mutual relations of science and Scripture till men make up their minds to do violence to neither, and to deal faithfully with both. On the very threshold, therefore, of such discussions as the present, we are encountered by the necessity for a candid, truthful, and impartial exegesis of the sacred text. This can never be honoured by being put to the torture. We ought to harbour no hankering after so-called 'reconciliations,' or "allow these to warp in the very least our rendering of the record. It is our business to decipher, not to prompt; to keep our ears open to what the Scripture says, not exercise our ingenuity on what it can be made to say. We must purge our minds at once of that order of prepossessions which is incident to an over-timid faith, and, not less scrupulously, of those counter prejudices which beset a jaundiced and captious scepticism. For there may be an eagerness to magnify, and even to invent difficulties, as well as an anxiety to muffle them up and smooth them over,— of which last, the least pleasing shape is an affectation of contempt disguising obvious perplexity and trepidation. Those who seek the repose of truth had best banish from the quest of it, in whatever field, the spirit and the methods of sophistry. The geologist, for example, if loyal to his science, will marshal his facts as if there were no book of Genesis. Even so is it the duty of the interpreter of the Mosaic text to fix its sense and investigate its structure, as though it were susceptible of neither collation nor collision with any science of geology."— *Replies*, p. 277.

"Let the interpreter then resolve, with God's assisting grace, to be candid and truthful. Let him fear not to state honestly the results of his own honest investigations; let him be simple, reverent, and plain-spoken, and above all, let him pray against that sectarian bias which, by importing its own foregone conclusions into the word of Scripture, and by refusing to see or to

"acknowledge what makes against its own pre-
"judices, has proved the greatest known hindrance
"to all fair interpretation, and has tended, more
"than anything else in the world, to check the
"free course of Divine Truth. . . . . It is indeed
"a cause for devout thankfulness, if not even for
"a recognition of a special providence, that out of
"the vast number of various readings so few affect
"vital questions; still it is indisputably a fact that
"but few pages of the New Testament can be
"turned over without our finding points of the
"greatest interest affected by very trivial varia-
"tions of reading. . . . .

"There are, alas! still many signs of uneasiness
"and obstruction; but we do entreat and conjure
"those who would only too gladly put the whole
"question in abeyance, to pause, seriously to pause,
"before they do such dishonour to the words of in-
"spiration. . . . . . Mournful, indeed, will be the
"retrospect, and gloomy indeed the future, if un-
"becoming anxiety or a timid conservatism is to
"tempt honest hearts to shew sadly lacking mea-
"sures of faith, and to deal deceitfully with the
"Oracles of God."—*Aids to Faith*, p. 421.

These extracts of course prove nothing as to
the general intention of the writers. Some of them
may be concessions reluctantly extorted, others
may be inconsistent with what they have said elsewhere, or even in the immediate context. But
I have quoted them for two reasons. First, as
a pledge and omen of peace. When passages like
these can be found, implying so close an agreement

of opinion between the assailant and assailed, it is clear that ultimate harmony cannot be distant between the candid and well-instructed of both sides, however far it may be removed between the mere ignorant partisans of either section. With such a common ground of feeling and expression on a topic admitting of so much dispute as that of Inspiration, it is evident that, as has been well said on another subject, if the human mind had as great a power of appreciating agreement as it has of appreciating differences, the controversy would be at an end. These passages, whilst they do not prove unqualified unanimity between the several distinguished persons in question, do prove both sides to be agreed in this—first, that the Bible is inspired; but, secondly, that it is not inspired in such a sense as to preclude human imperfection, not in such a sense as is required by the Helvetic Confession, or by the many excellent men amongst ourselves, who unfortunately profess to regard the admission of the least error in the Sacred Volume as inconsistent with the communion of the Church of England, or even with a belief in the Christian religion. Secondly, these passages, so expressed and so sanctioned, shew that, whatever may be the immediate result of prosecutions and attacks on particular individuals, the general and final conclusion is certain. The tide of speculation may pass beyond the principles here laid down, but it can never recede behind them. We shall not be forced to part with the belief that " *God spake*" *in the Bible*, "*by the Prophets, and by His Son;*" but neither shall we be forced to part with the belief that "*He spake at sundry times and in divers manners.*" "The treatment of the Bible according to a theory "of literal inspiration, which would make every "theology impossible [c]," can henceforth be no more imposed on the English Church.

It has lately been said that on the maintenance or rejection of this theory depends the acceptance or rejection of the whole Bible. Such an expectation is contrary to the whole previous analogy of the history of Christian doctrine. The hypothesis of a literal and uniform inspiration was not held by those of the Fathers whose lives were most devoted to the study of the Bible—Jerome and Chrysostom. It was not held by the first Reformers, Erasmus, Luther, and Calvin, who restored the study of the Bible to Western Europe. It was not held by those German divines[d] from whom has proceeded the main impulse to the study and interpretation of the Bible in modern Christendom. With a very few exceptions, it is not held by those who have most ardently and successfully pursued Biblical criticism in England or in France[e]. If it be true that even

[c] I quote from the work of the great Roman Catholic divine of Germany, "The Church and the Churches," by Dr. Döllinger, p. 162.
[d] See this well set forth in Dr. Pusey's "Theology of Germany," Part II. c. 5.
[e] See an excellent Article on the subject by M. Pressensè in the *Revue Chrétienne*, November, 1862.

now there is amongst theological students a very imperfect knowledge of the Scriptures compared with that which is possessed on other subjects, yet it is certain that this knowledge is much more considerable than it was twenty years ago; and that of all branches of theological study it is the one which has made the greatest progress, contemporaneously with the growth of that freedom of inquiry which has, happily, till within the last few years been allowed to advance without any sudden or violent check.

The main end to be sought is an increased acquaintance with the Bible, and increased appreciation of its instructions. By these, more than by any other means, will all theories of Inspiration find their true solution. This is the hope which I have laboured to set forth in these Sermons, and which I would wish here once for all to express briefly in the well-known language of two of the best amongst our living divines:—

"Christendom needed a firm spot on which she "might stand, and has found it in the Bible. Had "the Bible been drawn up in precise statements of "faith, or detailed precepts of conduct, we should "have had no alternative but either permanent "subjection to an outer law, or loss of the highest "instrument of self-education. But the Bible, from "its very form, is exactly adapted to our present "want. Even the perverted use of it has not "been without certain great advantages. And "meanwhile how utterly impossible it would be

"in the manhood of the world to imagine any
"other instructor of mankind. And for that
"reason, every day makes it more and more evi-
"dent that the thorough study of the Bible, the
"investigation of what it teaches and what it does
"not teach, the determination of the limits of
"what we mean by its inspiration, the determina-
"tion of the degree of authority to be ascribed
"to the different books, if any degrees are to be
"admitted, must take the lead of all other studies.
"Even the mistakes of careful and reverent stu-
"dents are more valuable now than truth held in
"unthinking acquiescence. The substance of the
"teaching which we derive from the Bible will not
"really be affected by anything of this sort; while
"its hold upon the minds of believers, and its
"power to stir the depths of the spirit of man,
"however much weakened at first, must be im-
"measurably strengthened in the end, by clearing
"away any blunders which may have been fastened
"on it by human interpretation.

"The immediate work of our day is the study
"of the Bible. Other studies will act upon the
"progress of mankind by acting through and upon
"this. For while a few highly educated men here
"and there who have given their minds to special
"pursuits may think the study of the Bible a thing
"of the past, yet assuredly, if their science is to
"have its effect upon men in the mass, it must be
"by affecting their moral and religious convictions;
"in no other way have men been, or can men be,
"deeply and permanently changed."

"Those who hold the possibility of a recon-

"cilement or restoration of belief, are anxious to
"preserve the historical use of Scripture as the
"continuous witness in all ages of the higher things
"in the heart of man, as the inspired source of
"truth and the way to the better life. They are
"willing to take away some of the external sup-
"ports, because they are not needed and do harm;
"also, because they interfere with the meaning.
"They have a faith, not that after a period of
"transition all things will remain just as they were
"before, but that they will all come round again
"to the use of man and to the glory of God.
"When interpreted like any other book, by the
"same rules of evidence and the same canons of
"criticism, the Bible will still remain unlike any
"other book; its beauty will be freshly seen, as
"of a picture which is restored after many ages
"to its original state; it will create a new interest
"and make for itself a new kind of authority by
"the life which is in it. It will be a spirit and
"not a letter; as it was in the beginning, having
"an influence like that of the spoken word, or the
"book newly found. The purer the light in the
"human heart, the more it will have an expression
"of itself in the mind of Christ; the greater the
"knowledge of the development of man, the truer
"will be the insight gained into the 'increasing
"'purpose' of Revelation. In which also the indi-
"vidual soul has a practical part, finding a sym-
"pathy with its own imperfect feelings, in the
"broken utterances of the Psalmist or the Prophet,
"as well as in the fulness of Christ. The harmony
"between Scripture and the life of man in all its

" stages may be far greater than appears at pre-
" sent. There, a world weary of the heat and dust
" of controversy, of speculations about God and
" man, weary, too, of the rapidity of its own mo-
" tion, would return home and find rest."

SERMON I.

God spake at sundry times and in divers manners.

PREACHED IN CHRIST CHURCH CATHEDRAL,
ON THE TWENTY-SECOND SUNDAY AFTER TRINITY,
Nov. 4, 1860.

SERMON I.

HEBREWS i. 1, 2.

God, who at sundry times and in divers manners spake in time past unto the fathers by the prophets, hath in these last days spoken unto us by His Son.

IN the Psalms for this morning's service, there are a few well-known verses, which, though relating in the first instance to a portion only of the Old Testament, yet convey a true description of the whole Bible. "The law of the Lord is an undefiled "law, converting the soul: the testimony of the "Lord is sure, and giveth wisdom unto the simple. "The statutes of the Lord are right, and rejoice the "heart: the commandment of the Lord is pure, and "giveth light unto the eyes. The fear of the Lord is "clean, and endureth for ever: the judgments of "the Lord are true and righteous altogether. More "to be desired are they than gold, yea, than much "fine gold: sweeter also than honey and the honey-"comb. Moreover by them is Thy servant taught, "and in keeping of them there is great reward [a]."

To shew how this is true of the contents of the Bible, how profound a wisdom lies in its words, in its history, in its doctrines; how much its teaching has hitherto done for the world, how much it yet may do, belongs rather to all sermons than to any

[a] Ps. xix. 7—11.

one in particular. But it may be within the limits of a single discourse to point out how much may be learned even from its outward form and structure; how not merely from the Revelation which it contains, but from the mode in which that Revelation is given, it is fitted to be the guide of theological study, fitted not merely to "rejoice the heart" and "convert the soul," but "to give light unto the "eyes and wisdom unto the simple." And if in this short statement I can allay any needless alarm, or satisfy any innocent doubt, or induce any one student to value his Bible more truly, or persuade any two opponents to find a common standing-ground beyond what they thought for, my purpose will be answered.

I propose, then, for the sake of convenience, to take as an outline of what I have to say, the very expressive words of my text; which, though they were written before the completion of the Sacred Volume, yet describe with singular fidelity its general characteristic. I quote them in the order in which they stand in the original Greek. "In *sundry* "times and in *divers* manners, in time past God "spoke unto the fathers *in the Prophets*, and in "these last days spoke unto us *in His Son*."

"In sundry times," that is, *in many parts*,—"in "divers manners," that is, *in many modes*—πολυμερῶς καὶ πολυτρόπως. This is the grand outward distinction of the Divine Revelation—applicable mainly to the Old Testament, but in a sufficient sense to the New Testament also. It is a truth which our carnal understanding and unenlightened reason is unwilling to admit: but which, the moment it is appreciated, solves innumerable difficulties. Like the roll given to the Prophet [b], though bitter in the mouth at first, it becomes, when eaten, sweeter than honey and the honeycomb. As in the case of the Apostle, out of what seems at first sight the weakness of Scripture, comes its most enduring strength; when it is most weak, then it is indeed most strong [c].

In order to bring out fully and distinctly this characteristic of our sacred Book, it will be useful to contrast it throughout with what others esteem their sacred book. For this purpose it will be useful to take that which is next in dignity and importance, the Koran of Mahometanism, and to ask wherein the Bible differs from it—(not, I repeat, in authority or doctrine—this would be superfluous,) but in the outward appearance and structure by which our attention is challenged to it, even before we open it. Grant the excellence of the Koran to the very utmost,—concede to it all that has ever been claimed for it,—still the differences which I am about to mention serve to bring out the contrast between what the Bible would be, if narrowed down to our puny measurements, and what, in its own divine and universal excellence, it actually is.

1. The Koran is absolutely uniform in style and mode of expression. It reflects the mind of one single person. It is as the Old Testament might

The diversity of style.

[b] Ezek. iii. 3, 4.   [c] 2 Cor. xii. 10.

be if it were composed by the single Prophet Isaiah, or the New Testament if it were composed by the single Apostle St. Paul. It is what the whole Bible would be, if from its pages were excluded all individual personalities, all human elements, all differences of time and place and character. But it is not so. The Bible is the composition not of one person, but of many. It is full of the most varied incidents. The styles of its different authors are marked beyond the possibility of mistake.

Out of this diversity arise some of its chief instruction. On the face of each book, we see what each book was intended to be, and to teach. The order and succession of St. Paul's Epistles (to take a single instance) is in itself a sermon. In each portion of each book we see what is prose and what is poetry; what is primeval history and what is later history; what is allegory, or parable, or drama, and what is chronicle, or precept, or narrative. Follow out the account thus given of itself by each part of Scripture, and you cannot go far wrong. The Bible in this way is not only its own interpreter, but its own guide. To read as history what was meant for parable, to read as precept what was meant for warning, is indeed striving to be wise above that which is written. The styles of Scripture are, as it were, so many heaven-planted sign-posts to set our faith in the right direction. And not only so, but from this manifold wisdom of the Bible, " many coloured " ($\pi o \lambda v \pi o i \kappa \iota \lambda o s$) as the Apostle calls it, arises its singular power of addressing each individual as if he were the very person spoken of in this or that book or chapter; "like the eye of "a portrait," as has been described in a well-known passage, "uniformly fixed upon us, turn where we "will." There is no other book, which, when opened at random, has so often returned an appropriate answer to the inquirer. For there is no other book, sacred or profane, which, within so short a compass, expresses the thoughts and feelings of so many different minds and situations. It is not a continual rhapsody, like the Koran; it is not a continual hymn, like the Veda: we have but to listen with an attentive ear, and we hear the Scriptures speaking to us, "every man in our "own tongue wherein we were born, the wonder- "ful works of God[d]."

2. The Koran represents not merely one single person, but one single scene and phase of society. It is, with a very few exceptions, purely Arabian. It is what the Bible would be if all external influences were obliterated, and it represented one single exclusive phase of Jewish life. But *our* Sacred Book, however Jewish and Oriental in its origin, is a stream formed of the confluence of many tributaries. Even the scenery and the life of Palestine were far more diversified than those of Arabia, so that whilst the Koran contains hardly any allusions except to the phenomena of the desert, the Bible includes topics which come home to almost every condition and position of life. The sea,

The diversity of scene.

[d] Acts ii. 8, 11.

the mountain, the town; the pastoral, the civilized, the republican, the royal state, can all find expression in its words. And not only so, but Egypt, Chaldæa, Persia, Greece, Rome, all came into contact with its gradual formation, so that alone of all sacred books it avowedly includes the words, and thoughts, and forms of other religions than its own —alone of all Oriental books, it has an actual affinity of aspect and form with the Northern and the Western world—alone almost of religious books, its story is constantly traversing the haunts of the world at large. The Koran, the Vedas, even Thomas à Kempis and St. Augustine, "*stay at home.*" But the Bible is a book that travels far and wide. "The " whole Epistle," says Bengel of one of the letters of St. Paul, "itinerarium sapit." The whole of the Bible, it might almost be said, is one continued journeying to and fro. By sea and land, by valley and mountain, by its coincidences, by its dangers, by its escapes, it is the companion of every traveller, however cosmopolite; read even when not believed; necessary, even when unwelcome. " It goeth " forth from the uttermost part of the heaven, and " runneth about unto the end of it again, and there " is nothing hid from the heat thereof."

Even independent of its higher consolations, by the very fact of its ubiquity what a treasure must such a Book have been to the world,—what a bond of union between East and West, between Jew and Gentile! Those traces of other nations and other religions in its sacred pages, which some timid

Christians have tried to exorcise as though they were unhallowed intruders into the sacred ground, by how many additional links do they attach the Bible to the great names and places of the human race! what a solidity, what a breadth have they given both to its evidences and to its doctrine! what an indication of its lofty purpose, of its universal aims!

3. The Koran prides itself on its *perfection* of composition—on its freedom from all blemishes of diction or statement. Its pure Arabic style is regarded as a proof of its divinity. To translate it into other languages is esteemed by orthodox Mussulmen as impiety, and when it is translated its beauty is lost. It is maintained to be in every word and point a transcript of the Divine original. Mahomet represented himself as literally the "sacred penman." Till quite recently it was forbidden to be printed even in Arabic, lest any of the sacred letters should be injured. Such is the strength of the Koran. In far other and opposite quarters lies the strength of the Bible. True, its sacred text is uncertain; and this uncertainty is adduced by Mahometans as a cogent argument in their disputes with Christian missionaries. True; but the Christian missionary, if he be well instructed in his own religion, will reply that the Divine authority, which in the Koran is ascribed to the words and syllables, is in the Bible far more deeply rooted. The various readings which in the Koran were suppressed once for all by the Caliph

marginal note: The diversity of language.

Othman, have broken out freely by thousands and thousands over the whole face of the Christian Scriptures: the stumbling-blocks here and there of faithless disciples, but the delight of Christian scholarship, the safeguards of Christian doctrine, the relics of Christian antiquity. True, we have been so free with the sacred words as to allow them to range through hundreds of versions; running the risk of false and partial readings for the chance of their wider diffusion. Even the Apostles used the Septuagint instead of the original, in spite of its manifold deviations: we ourselves use two translations of the Psalter, side by side, of which neither agrees with the other. But the Bible has stood the process. Hebrew poetry, as often observed, instead of repelling translation, by its freedom from rhyme and metre absolutely invites it. The New Testament alone, it has been said, of ancient books, actually gains by its re-appearance in the languages of England and Germany. So little does its force depend on its words, so mightily does its spirit work even through "the sundry times and divers manners" of modern, Gentile, Western nations.

And when we go back to the original itself, the same truth emerges yet again. Its language is not classical: in the Old Testament, it is the uncouth, unhewn, unartificial Hebrew; without particles, without conjunctions, without degrees of comparison: in the New Testament, it is not the pure Attic of Demosthenes, but the debased, corrupted, homely dialect of Hellenistic Greek.

But let us thank God that imperfection of grammar, of style, of expression, was not thought an unworthy vehicle of the teaching of His Spirit. These very imperfections, these very inaccuracies, fitted the sacred languages for the task which they had to perform.

Beautifully has this adaptation been portrayed by our two highest authorities on each of the two Scriptural languages. "The words of judgment "bursting out, one by one, slowly, heavily, con-"densed, abrupt, from the Prophet's heavy and "shrinking soul;" "each sentence wrung forth with "a groan, as though he had anew to take breath be-"fore he uttered a renewed woe; each word forming "a whole for itself, like one heavy toll in a funeral "knell." This is the bold, but not too bold, description (by one who knows it well[c]) of the rough, disjointed, yet sublime style of the Hebrew Prophet. And of the Greek of the New Testament it has been said with equal reverence and equal force:—"At the "time when our Saviour came into the world the "Greek language was in a state of degeneracy and "decay. But that degeneracy may be ranked among "the causes that fanned the growth of Christianity. "It was a preparation for the Gospel; the decaying "soil in which the new elements of life were to come "forth; the one common speech of the then civilized "nations of the world. The definiteness of earlier "forms of human speech would have imposed a limit "on the freedom of the Gospel. A religion which

[c] Professor Pusey's Commentary on Hosea, pp. 5, 6.

"was to be universal required that the division of "languages, no less than of nations, should be "broken down. It pleased God, through broken "and hesitating forms of speech, with no beauty "or comeliness of style, to reveal the universal truth "for which the Greek of Plato would have been no "fitting temple '."

The diversity of materials. 4. The Koran claims not only a perfection of style, but a uniform completeness of materials. It incorporates in itself no earlier documents; it has no degrees (or hardly any) of authority in its several chapters; it contains the whole religion of Islam within itself. In all these points, again, the Bible takes its stand on what some would deem a lower level, but on what experience has proved to be a far higher. Its contents are like a vast quarry rather than a finished building: we find the rough materials with which the edifice must be reconstructed, the solid marble and the precious metal, sometimes on the surface, sometimes far below. We must not be ashamed to dig for it; by the sweat of our brow, by the toil of our brain, must we eat our spiritual as well as our bodily food:

> "Pater ipse colendi
> Haud facilem esse viam voluit."

It is this which makes researches into the Bible so attractive, so suggestive, so inexhaustible. Its contradictions and variations; the large variations of the Septuagint from the Hebrew text; the

---

' Professor Jowett's Commentary on St. Paul, i. p. 135. Essays and Reviews, p. 390.

well-known discrepancies between the several Evangelists, or between the Books of Kings and Chronicles,—how invaluable as a Divine witness to the great Evangelical doctrine that the spirit is above the letter, the whole above the parts, the end above the means [g]! Its scattered portions of truth, not gathered in one place, but lying here and there; the history eked out by Psalmists and Prophets; the Acts supported and corrected by the Epistles; fragments in the Chronicles fitting into a vacant place in the Books of Exodus or Kings,—what a stimulant to industry, what an exercise for judgment, what a sanction to those modern arts of study, by which these treasures have been first discovered and put together!

[g] Take the single instance of St. Stephen's speech in the Acts of the Apostles. It is a summary of the Old Testament history; yet, in almost every incident which it quotes, it contains a variation from the sacred text. There are no less than seven remarkable discrepancies or additions of this kind. It is just possible that for each one of these an explanation may be imagined or invented. But this does not make the variation itself less remarkable. If the Bible were what we in our later theories have supposed it to be,—" every book of it, every chapter of it, every verse of it, every word of it, every letter of it, the direct utterance of the Most High, . . . absolute, faultless, unerring, supreme,"—then every one of those variations would be as great a crime as Stephen's denunciations of the local worship of the temple were in the eyes of the Jews. But, because the Bible is to be viewed, not by our theories concerning it, but by what it says of itself, therefore the speech of Stephen, so far from being a difficulty, is an immense advantage, in shewing us that already in the Apostolic age the stress was laid not on its letter but its spirit, not on its form but its substance, and that the form and the letter are repeatedly altered and varied as if to impress upon us this very truth.

The diversity of effects.

The lessons of this divine incompleteness may be carried yet a step further. The Koran is to the Mussulman, in one sense, even more than the Bible is to the Christian. It is his code of laws, his liturgy, his creed. The Bible, on the other hand, needs, for its full effect, the institutions, the teaching, the society of Christendom. Its truths are capable of expansion, diffusion, progression, far beyond the mere circumference of the volume which contains them. "The Word of God," as the Apostle says, "is not bound" in its own fetters.

The lives and deeds—above all, the One vast Life and Work—which it records, spread their influence almost irrespectively of the words in which they were first recorded. The Bible propagates itself by other means than multiplication of its written or printed copies. Creeds, as has been sometimes said, are Bibles in miniature; sacred pictures have been often and truly called the Bibles of the unlearned. "Ye are my epistle," said the Apostle to his converts[h]; Christians are, or ought to be, the living Bibles of the world. The false religion begins and ends in a Sacred Book; the true religion is founded on a Sacred Life, and ends in a Sacred Spirit. It is not in the close limitation of the stream to its parent spring, but in the wide overflow of its waters, that the true fountain of Biblical inspiration shews its divine abundance and vitality.

5. The Koran, with a few exceptions, is stationary. It is literally one book, and it is a book

[h] 2 Cor. iii. 2.

(for the most part) without coherence, without sequence, without advance.

On the other hand, the vast variety of the Bible, of which I have already spoken, would lose half its interest unless it were also progressive. Each successive revelation, dispensation, and manifestation which its pages contain is partial, incomplete, and imperfect, because it is superseded by some fuller and higher revelation which grows out of it. It is not one Testament, but two; not one book, but many. It has been scornfully said[i] that it is now too late to view the books of the Bible as separate from each other. " Too late" is a word alarmingly true in worldly politics; but it is a word that has no place in Christian theology, any more than in Christian practice. It never can be too late " rightly " to divide the word of truth" into its separate parts. Nor is it too late. Here, as elsewhere, what is called new is very old, as old as the Sacred Volume itself. There are two names by which the volume is called, expressing the double truth concerning it. One is the present modern name, " *the Bible,*" which was first introduced in the thirteenth century, and which expresses by a happy solecism the general unity of form and design that runs through all its pages. But the names by which it was known in earlier times, and which are still its authorized and solemn titles, indicate no less clearly the plurality of its books. Αἱ Γράφαι, τὰ Βίβλια—the *Scriptures* —*Biblia Sacra;* these are the names by which for

The diversity of revelations.

---

[i] Westminster Review, (October, 1860).

the first twelve hundred years of the Church the manifold divisions of the Bible were signified to the humblest reader. Book after book, Scripture after Scripture, Psalm after Psalm, Epistle after Epistle, each with its own sacred message, go to make up the still more sacred whole.

"O fools and slow of heart" if, by confounding them altogether, we miss the special purpose and occasion of each! O happy, thrice happy, if we did but recognise our own good gifts; if we would but thankfully observe how God has tempered the whole together, so that "those parts which we think "less honourable, on those He has bestowed more "abundant honour;" if only we will remember that each has its appointed task—that "the foot is not the "hand, nor the eye the ear." "If the whole Bible "were seeing, where were the hearing; or if the "whole were hearing, where were the smelling[k]?"

Bishop Warburton perhaps pushed his argument to excess when he endeavoured to prove the Divine Legation of Moses, by shewing the absence of any doctrine of a future state in the Mosaic law. Yet within certain limits the argument admits of a sound and a wide application. The blanks, the silences, the pauses, the defects, of the sacred Books are often as necessary and as wholesome as their fulness, perfection, and eloquence. The Book of Esther never names the name of God. Shall we on that account cast it out of the Canon? Shall we not rather hail it as a blessed assurance that the

[k] 1 Cor. xii. 17, 23.

Spirit of God may be found where His Name is not, as surely as it often is not found where His Name is? The Book of Ecclesiastes is full of distraction and despondency. God be praised that at least in one Book of the Bible the cries of doubt and perplexity which man refuses to hear have reached the ears of the Lord of Sabaoth, and not been shut out from His written Word! The Epistle of St. James, in direct contravention of the theological language of later days, says that "a man is not justified by "faith only[1]:" is it therefore to be rejected as "an "Epistle of straw," or is it not rather the very book we need for the completion of Apostolical truth, and the correction of our own theories?

And when from particular instances we turn to the effect of the whole, the lesson both becomes more distinct and more widely useful. We see the gradual dawn. We read the express announcement of the fact in the successive declarations of Scripture itself. "I spake not unto your fathers concerning "burnt-offerings or sacrifices," says Jeremiah of the ceremonial Law[m]; "I will avenge the blood "of Jezreel," is the word of Hosea upon Jehu[n]. "The son shall not bear the iniquity of the father," says Ezekiel of the second commandment[o]. "The law "came by Moses, but grace and truth by Jesus Christ," says St. John[p], in contrasting the old and the new dispensations. "A shadow of things to come, but "the body is of Christ," says St. Paul[q]. "The law

---

[1] St. James ii. 24.   [m] Jer. vii. 22.   [n] Hos. i. 4.
[o] Ezek. xviii. 20.   [p] St. John i. 17.   [q] Col. ii. 17.

"was a shadow of good things to come," says the author of the Epistle to the Hebrews[r]. "Many pro-"phets and kings desired to see the things which "ye see, and have not seen them," says our Lord Himself. "Moses, because of the hardness of your "hearts, suffered you to put away your wives." "Moses gave you not that bread from Heaven[s]." "Ye have heard that it hath been said by them, "Hate your enemy; but I say unto you, Love "your enemies[t]."

How completely do passages like these acknowledge, and by acknowledging solve, the difficulty of the inferiority of the earlier Revelations to the later! How completely do the words of my text tell us, on the one hand, that it was "to our *fathers*," and not *to us*, that "God spoke in times past;" and yet, on the other hand, that it was the voice of God to them, although in different tones from those which He uses now. It was a great misfortune for Christian theology when, in the days of the Puritans, all the laws and precepts of the Old Testament were considered binding on Christian men. But it would be an almost equal misfortune, for the prospects of enlightened knowledge no less than of religious zeal, if the Old Testament with its manifold instructions ceased to be valued and studied amongst us, in connection with the Christian Scriptures. It is this very connection, this sanction in spite of differences, which furnishes the best example of that great truth, so distasteful to the unrenewed intellect

[r] Heb. x. 1.   [s] St. John vi. 32.   [t] St. Matt. v. 43, 44.

and the unregenerate heart,—the truth, namely, that ages, nations, churches, individuals must be judged, not by our standard but by theirs; not by the light which they have not, but by the light which they have. Considering the immense difficulty and also the immense importance (for all purposes of instruction and intelligence) of impressing this truth on the uneducated and the half-educated, we can hardly over-rate the possible use of the Bible in this respect.

There is a well-known congregation in the east of London in which not long ago the preacher was interrupted by loud and tumultuous signs of disapproval, because he stated that " in matters of re-"ligion there must be differences of opinion," and that " we ought to put ourselves in our opponent's "point of view." To feelings like these, and to that far more numerous class of which they are the rough representatives, reason of course speaks in vain and philosophy is a word unknown. But the Bible, even with these, is still a recognised authority, and it is a pledge and hope for the future that the large and generous principle to which the passions of men are so vehemently opposed is the very principle of which not merely the doctrines of the Bible are full, but on which its very framework and existence is built up and held together.

6. There remains the concluding, but extensive, lesson to which this day's Epistle calls our attention—the duty, amidst a Book so manifold, of

"proving the things that are excellent,"—δοκιμάζειν τὰ διαφέροντα,—distinguishing the important from the unimportant.

The diversity of proportions. In saying this, I under-rate no portion of the sacred volume. There are those (and I thankfully count myself amongst their number) to whom infinite and unfeigned delight is imparted by a chapter of geographical names in the Book of Joshua, the dark story of Rizpah the daughter of Aiah, or of Ishmael the son of Nethaniah. Study and examine these portions,—the more, the better. But the whole tenor of the Bible forbids us to raise them to the same level as the Prophecies of Isaiah or the Sermon on the Mount. We cannot mistake the emphasis with which the progressive Revelation accentuates (so to say) the leading episodes and characters which it discloses. Most useful is this intimation even in its most general aspect. We can never be too often reminded that there is a sacred doctrine of *proportion* in all things, divine as well as human. Truth is one, as light is one. But light has its many colours, and truth has its many shades, its many degrees, its many aspects. To track out these several shades lightening ever more and more into the perfect day would be most edifying even had we no distinct landmarks to guide us. Such landmarks we have in abundance. I confine myself to two—those two which are named in the text, and which shall be followed out at length hereafter.

"He spake *by the Prophets.*" This one word

taken in its full original sense, and in all its bearings on the history, is the key to the main purpose of the Old Testament. Fix your eye on the Prophets, not only in their writings, but their lives; observe wherein the Prophetical office consisted, and why it was of such supreme value to the Jewish Church, and through them to all mankind. The spirit of the Prophets is the spirit of the Old Testament, indeed of the whole Bible.

"He hath in these last days spoken to us *by* "*His Son*." This opens a still wider field. It reveals the centre of the New Testament. It indicates the end to which the graduated, multiform, complex revelation of the Old Testament had been tending, and wherein it closed. This necessary gravitation, as it were, of the Jewish history to its final catastrophe is at once the sanction and the correction of the whole system of types and antitypes, prophecies and fulfilments of prophecy. We want a storehouse of illustrations for the Christian history, and we find them to our hand in the Jewish annals; we want a conclusion to the Jewish history worthy of its great beginning, and we find it beyond question in the greatest event of all history. Consciously or unconsciously, the characters and writings of the rest of the Bible fall into their relative places around the Gospel history, as surely as, in that history itself, the soldiers, priests, disciples, Jews, and Romans derive their interest and significance from being grouped round the central Figure and round the Cross on Calvary. Take away that

Figure, take away that Cross, and the background of the Old Testament as well as the foreground of the New Testament become dull and colourless, as when the sun has gone down. Of all the characteristics of the Sacred Volume, none is more pregnant with instruction than that by which the Gospel history thus takes its place above the rest of the Bible,—above the Prophets of the Old Testament, above the Epistles of the New Testament.

And O! my brethren, if any of us have any doubt about any part of the Bible, or if any of us be eager to answer any doubts in others, first and before all things learn the mind and spirit of CHRIST as set forth in the four Gospels. In that mind and spirit lies the true solution of all our disputes about the nature of the Infinite. In that mind and spirit lies the true key to all the mysteries of His life and death,—the meaning of His miracles, the salt of His words, the virtue of His sacrifice, the power of His resurrection. It was a true feeling which gave to our religion the name of that one single pre-eminent portion of the Sacred Volume —the GOSPEL. It was a true feeling which led the Fathers to take, as the subject of the Creeds, the one doctrine which above all others belongs to the Gospels, namely, the INCARNATION.

To those who are weary of controversy, to those who are laden with perplexities, to those who travail and labour with the hardness, or the dulness, or the indifference of men, no less than to the suffering and the mourners, there is one and the same exhortation of which the fulness of meaning still remains, and will long remain, unexhausted,— "Hear what comfortable words our Saviour Christ "saith to all that truly turn to Him: 'Come unto "'Me all ye that labour and are heavy laden, and "'I will give you rest.'"

SERMON II.

God spake by the Prophets.

PREACHED IN ST. MARY'S CHURCH,

On Feb. 9, 1862.

SERMON II.[a]

HEBREWS i. 1.

God spake by the Prophets.

IN my former discourse on this subject I called the attention of this congregation to the former part of this verse, as describing those peculiarities in the *form* of the Bible which distinguish it from all other Sacred Books. It is my intention on the present occasion to dwell on the second part of the verse, describing the peculiarity of *spirit* which distinguishes the whole Bible, but in a special degree the Old Testament.

"God spake by the Prophets." The author of the Epistle had in the words immediately preceding spoken of the various gradations of revelation, and then fixes our attention on the instructors or revealers of God's will, who stood on the highest step of those gradations. These are, in one word, the *Prophets.* There can be no one in this place to whom the historical portions of the Old Testament are more precious than they are to me; but I cannot refuse to acknowledge the limitation of the Sacred Text which says that "God spake," not by the

[a] This Sermon was preceded by a Lecture delivered on the previous day, on the History of the Prophetical Order. I have inserted so much of this Lecture in the early part of the Sermon as was necessary to complete the argument.

historians, geographers, chronologers, but in a special sense " by the Prophets." And again, although the full sense of the word " Inspiration" is that in which alone our Church has used it, as applying to the Universal Church, and to every good thought and work of the human heart; yet there is a deep truth in the third clause of the Nicene Creed, "I " believe in the Holy Ghost, who spake" (not by Bishops, or Presbyters, or General Councils, or General Assemblies, but) " by the Prophets."

This limitation or concentration of the Divine Inspiration to the Prophetic spirit is in exact accordance with the facts of the case. The Prophets being, as their name both in Greek and Hebrew implies, the most immediate organ of the will of God, it is in their utterances, if anywhere, that we must expect to find the most direct expression of that will. However high the sanction given to King or Priest in the Old dispensation, they were always to bow before the authority of the Prophet. The Prophetic teaching is, as it were, the essence of the Revelation, sifted from its accidental accompaniments. It pervades and, by pervading, gives its own vitality to those portions of the Sacred Volume which cannot strictly be called Prophetical. Josephus speaks of the *succession* (διαδοχὴ) of the Prophets, as constituting the main framework and staple of the Sacred Canon of the Old Testament. What has been beautifully said of the Psalms as compared with the Levitical and sacrificial system is still more true of the Prophets. "As we watch

"the weaving of the web, we endeavour to trace
"through it the more conspicuous threads. Long
"time the eye follows the crimson—it disappears at
"length: but the golden thread of sacred prophecy
"stretches to the end." It stretches to the end:
for it is the chief outward link between the Old
and the New Testament; and though the New
Testament has its own peculiarities, yet the Spirit
of Prophecy, though expressing chiefly the spirit of
the Old Testament, may also fitly be called the
spirit of the whole Bible.

Of the outward forms of the Prophetic teaching
I have already spoken elsewhere. It will be here
my duty to speak of the inward spirit of the Prophetic order,—to ask what there is in it which gave
to the Jewish people that element of progression
and elevation, which is the best proof of the Divine
authority of the Old Testament itself, and of its
practical use for us?

The very name of "Prophet" is expressive of its great design. If the derivation of the word, as commonly given, be correct—the "boiling or bubbling "over" of the Divine Fountain of Inspiration within the soul—it is impossible to imagine a phrase more expressive of the truth which it conveys. It is one of those words which conveys a host of imagery and doctrine in itself. In the most signal instances of the sites chosen for the Grecian oracles, we find that they were marked by the rushing forth of a living spring from the recesses of the native rocks of Greece, the Castalian spring at Delphi, the rushing

Importance of the office of the Prophets.

stream of the Hercyna at Lebadea. It was felt that nothing could so well express the Divine voice speaking from the mysterious abysses of the unseen world, as those inarticulate but lively ebullitions of the life-giving element from its unknown mysterious sources. Such a figure was even more significant in the remoter East. The prophetic utterances were indeed the bubbling, teeming springs of life in those hard primitive rocks, in those dry parched levels. "My heart," to use the phrase of the Psalmist in the original language[b], "is bursting, bubbling over "with a good matter." That is the very image which would be drawn from the abundant crystal fountains which all along the valley of the Jordan pour forth their full-grown streams, scattering fertility and verdure as they flow, over the rough ground. And this is the exact likeness of the springs of prophetic wisdom and foresight, containing in themselves and their accomplishment the fulness of the stream which was to roll on and fertilise the ages.

The existence of such an institution in the midst of an Eastern nation, even if we knew nothing of its teaching, must be regarded as a rare guarantee for liberty, for progress, for protection against wrong and falsehood. Even of the modern Dervishes, with all their drawbacks, it has been said, that "without them no man would be safe. They "are the chief people in the East, who keep in the "recollection of Oriental despots that there are

[b] Ps. xlv. 1.

" ties between heaven and earth. They restrain
" the tyrant in his oppression of his subjects; they
" are consulted by courts and by the counsellors of
" state in times of emergency; they are, in fact,
" the great benefactors of the human race in the
" East c."

Such, in relation to the mere brute power of the kings of Judah and Israel, were the Jewish Prophets,— constant, vigilant, watch-dogs d on every kind of abuse and crime, even in the highest ranks, by virtue of that universal, and at the same time elevated, position which belonged to the whole order. But they were much more than this. A great philosophical writer of our own time has thus set forth the position of the Hebrew Prophets e :—

" The Egyptian hierarchy, the paternal despotism
" of China, were very fit instruments for carrying
" those nations up to the point of civilization which
" they attained. But having reached that point,
" they were brought to a permanent halt, for want
" of mental liberty and individuality,—requisites
" of improvement which the institutions that had
" carried them thus far entirely incapacitated them
" from acquiring, and as the institutions did not
" break down and give place to others, further im-
" provement stopped. In contrast with these na-
" tions, let us consider the example of an opposite
" character, afforded by another and a compara-
" tively insignificant Oriental people—the Jews.

c Dr. Wolff's Travels. d Isa. lvi. 2.
e Mill's Representative Government, 41, 42.

"They, too, had an absolute monarchy and a hier-
"archy. These did for them what was done for
"other Oriental races by their institutions—sub-
"dued them to industry and order, and gave them
"a national life. But neither their kings nor their
"priests ever obtained, as in those other countries,
"the exclusive moulding of their character. Their
"religion gave existence to an inestimably precious
"unorganised institution, the *Order* (if it may be
"so termed) of Prophets. Under the protection,
"generally, though not always effectual, of their
"sacred character, the Prophets were a power in
"the nation, often more than a match for kings
"and priests, and kept up, in that little corner of
"the earth, the antagonism of influences which is
"the only real security for continued progress.
"Religion consequently was not there—what it
"has been in so many other places—a consecra-
"tion of all that was once established, and a barrier
"against further improvement. The remark of a
"distinguished Hebrew, that the Prophets were in
"Church and State the equivalent of the modern
"liberty of the press, gives a just but not an ade-
"quate conception of the part fulfilled in national
"and universal history by this great element of
"Jewish life; by means of which, the canon of in-
"spiration never being complete, the persons most
"eminent in genius and moral feeling could not
"only denounce and reprobate, with the direct
"authority of the Almighty, whatever appeared to
"them deserving of such treatment, but could give

"forth higher interpretations of the national religion, which thenceforth became part of the religion. Accordingly, whoever can divest himself of the habit of reading the Bible as if it was one book, which until lately was equally inveterate in Christians and in unbelievers, sees with admiration the vast interval between the morality and religion of the Pentateuch, or even of the historical books, and the morality and religion of the Prophecies, a distance as wide as between these last and the Gospels. Conditions more favourable to progress could hardly exist; accordingly, the Jews, instead of being stationary, like other Asiatics, were, next to the Greeks, the most progressive people of antiquity, and, jointly with them, have been the starting-point and main propelling agency of modern cultivation."

What then is the essence of this prophetic teaching? It may be divided into three parts, according to the three famous words of St. Bernard—*Respice, Aspice, Prospice.* The interpretation of the Divine Will respecting the Past, the Present, and the Future.

I. Of the Prophets as teachers of the experience of the Past we know but little. It is true that we have references to many of the books which they thus wrote. The acts of David, by Samuel, Gad, and Nathan; of Solomon and Jeroboam, by Nathan and Iddo; of Rehoboam, by Iddo and Shemaiah. But these unfortunately have all perished. Alas! As teachers of the Past.

of all the lost works of antiquity, is there any, heathen or sacred, to be named with the loss of the biography of David by the Prophet Nathan? We can, however, form some notion of these lost works by the fragments of historical writings that are left to us in the Prophetical Books of Isaiah and Jeremiah, and also by the likelihood that some of the present canonical books were founded upon the works which the compilation of the existing books must have tended to supersede. And it is probably not without some ground of this sort, that the Prophetical Books of the Old Testament, in the Jewish Canon, include the Books of Joshua, Judges, Samuel, and Kings. From these slight indications of the mission of the Prophets as historians, we cannot deduce any detailed instruction. But it is important to have at least this proof, that the study of history, so dear to some of us, and by some so lightly thought of, was not deemed beneath the notice of the Prophets of God. And if we may so far assume the ancient Jewish nomenclature as to believe that the historical books of the Canon just enumerated may be called "Prophetical," their structure furnishes topics well worthy of the consideration of the theological student. In that marvellously tessellated workmanship which they present,—in the careful interweaving of ancient documents into a later narrative,—in the editing and re-editing of passages, where the introduction of a more modern name or word betrays the touch of the more recent historian,—we trace a research which may well have occupied many a vacant hour in the prophetic schools of Bethel or Jerusalem, and at the same time a freedom of adaptation, of alteration, of inquiry, which places the authors or editors of these original writings on a level far above that of mere chroniclers or copyists. Such a union of restraint and freedom gives us, on the one hand, a view of the office of an inspired or prophetic historian, quite different from that which would degrade him into the brief and passive instrument of a power which effaced his individual energy and reflection; and, on the other hand, presents us with something like the model at which an historical student might well aspire even in our more modern age. And if, from the handiwork and composition of these writings, we reach to their substance, we find traces of the same spirit, which will appear more closely as we speak of the Prophetical Office in its two larger aspects. By comparing the treatment of the history of Israel or Judah in the four prophetical Books of Samuel and of Kings, with the treatment of the same subject in the Books of Chronicles, we are at once enabled to form some notion of the true characteristics of the Prophetical office as distinguished from that of the mere chronicler or Levite. But this will best be understood as we proceed.

II. I pass therefore to the work of the Prophets as interpreters of the Divine Will in regard to the Present. *As teachers of the Present.*

(1.) What was the characteristic of their directly

religious teaching which caused the early Fathers to regard them as, in the best sense of the word, "Theologians?"

The Unity of God. It consisted of two points—their proclamation of the Unity and of the Spirituality of the Divine Nature. They proclaimed the *Unity* of God, and hence the energy with which they attacked the falsehoods and superstitions which endeavoured to take the place of God. This was the negative side of their teaching, and the force with which they urge it, the withering scorn with which Elijah and Isaiah[f] speak of the idols of their time, however venerable, however sacred in the eyes of the worshippers, is a proof that even negative statements of theology may at times be needed, and have at any rate a standing place amongst the Prophetic gifts. The direct object of this negative teaching virtually expired with the immediate call for it under the Old Dispensation. *The Spirituality of God.* But the positive side of their teaching, the assertion of the *Spirituality*, the morality of God, His justice, His goodness, His love, continued to the very end, and received its highest development in the Prophets of the New Testament. Then the Prophetic teaching of the moral attributes of God were brought out more strongly than ever. Then Grace and Truth[g] were declared to be the only means of conceiving or approaching to the Divine Essence. Then He who was Himself the Incarnation of that Grace and Truth was enabled to say, as no Prophet before or

---

[f] 1 Kings xviii. 27; Isa. xliv. 16.   [g] St. John i. 14.

after could have said, "Ye believe in God, believe "also in Me[h]." To that crowning point of the Prophetic Theology, the Apostolic Prophets direct our attention so clearly, that no more need have been said on this subject. The doctrine of the Incarnation of Christ by the last of the Prophets, St. John, is the fitting and necessary close of the glimpse of the moral nature of the Divinity revealed to the first of the Prophets, Moses. This revelation of the Divine Essence, this manifestation of God in some unusually impressive form, constituted, as we have already seen, and shall see as we advance, at once the first call and the sustaining force of every Prophetic mission.

(2.) And now how is this foundation of the Prophetic Teaching carried out into detail? This brings us to the main characteristic of the Prophetic, as distinguished from all other parts of the Old Dispensation. The elevated conception of the Divinity may be said to pervade all parts of the Old Testament, if not in equal proportions, yet at least so distinctly as to be independent of any special office for its enforcement. But in the Prophetical teaching there is something yet more peculiarly its own.

The importance of Moral above Ceremonial Precepts.

The one great corruption to which all Religion is exposed, is its separation from morality. The very strength of the religious motive has a tendency to exclude, or disparage, all other tendencies of the human mind, even the noblest and best. It is against this corruption that the Prophetic Order

[h] St. John xiv. 1.

from first to last constantly protested. Even the mere outward appearance and organisation of the order bore witness to the greatness of the opposite truth of the inseparable union of morality and religion. Alone of all the high offices of the Jewish Church they were called by no outward form of consecration, and were selected from no special tribe or family. But the most effective witness to this great doctrine was borne by their actual teaching.

Amidst all their varieties, there is hardly a Prophet, from Samuel downwards, whose life or writings do not contain an assertion of this truth. It is to them as constant a topic, as the most peculiar and favourite doctrine of any eccentric sect or party is in the mouths of the preachers of such a sect or party at the present day, and it is rendered more forcible by the form which it takes of a constant protest against the sacrificial system of the Levitical ritual, which they either, in comparison with the Moral Law, disparage altogether, or else fix their hearers' attention to the moral and spiritual truth which lay behind it.

Listen to them one after another:—

Samuel.—" To obey is better than sacrifice, and " to hearken than the fat of rams[i]." *David.*— " Thou desirest not sacrifice; else would I give it. " Thou delightest not in burnt-offering. The sacri- " fices of God are a broken spirit. Sacrifice and " burnt-offering Thou didst not desire[j]. Then said

[i] 1 Sam. xv. 22.   [j] Ps. li. 16, 17, xl. 6—8.

"I, Lo, I come to do Thy will, O God." *Hosea.—* "I desired mercy, and not sacrifice [k]." *Amos.—*"I hate, I despise your feast days, and I will not smell in your solemn assemblies. Though ye offer Me burnt-offerings, and your meat-offerings, I will not accept them, neither will I regard the peace-offerings of your fat beasts. But let judgment run down as waters, and righteousness as a mighty stream [l]." *Micah.—*"Shall I come before the Lord with burnt-offerings, with calves of a year old? Will the Lord be pleased with thousands of rams, or with ten thousands of rivers of oil? shall I give my first-born for my transgression, the fruit of my body for the sin of my soul? He hath shewed thee, O man, what is good; and what doth the Lord require of thee, but to do justly, and to love mercy, and to walk humbly with thy God [m]?" *Isaiah.—*"Your new moons and your other feasts My soul hateth: they are a trouble to Me; I am weary to bear them. Wash you, make you clean; cease to do evil; learn to do well. Is not this the fast that I have chosen, to loose the bands of wickedness, to undo the heavy burdens, and to let the oppressed go free [n]?" *Jeremiah.—*"Amend your ways and your doings, and I will cause you to dwell in this place. Trust ye not in lying words, saying, The temple of the Lord, The temple of the Lord, The temple of the Lord, are these [o]." *Ezekiel.—*"If

---

[k] Hosea vi. 6.   [l] Amos v. 21.   [m] Micah vi. 6—8.
[n] Isa. i. 14, lviii. 15.   [o] Jer. vii. 3, 4.

"a man be just, and do that which is lawful and
"right, ... and hath executed true judgment be-
"tween man and man, hath walked in My statutes,
"and hath kept My judgments, to deal truly; he
"is just, he shall surely live.... The soul that
"sinneth, it shall die. The son shall not bear the
"iniquity of the father, neither the father the ini-
"quity of the son: the righteousness of the righte-
"ous shall be upon him, and the wickedness of the
"wicked shall be upon him.... When the wicked
"man turneth away from his wickedness that he
"hath committed, and doeth that which is lawful
"and right, he shall save his soul alive [p]."

Mercy and justice, judgment and truth, repentance and goodness—not sacrifice, not fasting, not ablutions, not local or hereditary sanctity—is the burden of the whole Prophetic teaching of the Old Testament. It is this which distinguishes the Prophetical from the Levitical portions even of the historical books. Compare the exaltation of moral duties in the Books of Kings with the exaltation of merely ceremonial duties in the Books of Chronicles, and the difference between the two elements of the Sacred History is at once apparent.

In the New Testament, the same doctrine is repeated in terms slightly altered, but still more emphatic. In the words of Him who is our Prophet in this the truest sense of all, I need only refer to the Sermon on the Mount [q], and to the remarkable fact that His chief warnings are against

[p] Ezek. xviii. 5—9, 20, 27, 28.   [q] St. Matt. v.—vii.

the ceremonial, the narrow, the religious world of that age[r]. In His deeds, I need only refer to His death—proclaiming as the very central fact and doctrine of the New Religion, that sacrifice, henceforth and for ever, consists not in the blood of bulls and goats[s], but in the perfect surrender of a perfect Will and Life to the perfect Will of an All Just and All Merciful God. In the Epistles the same Prophetic strain is still carried on by the elevation of the spirit above the letter[t], of love above all other gifts[u], of edification above miraculous signs[v], of faith and good works above the outward distinction of Jews and Gentiles[x]. With these accents on his lips[y], the Last of the Prophets expired.

It is this assertion of the supremacy of the moral and spiritual above the literal, the ceremonial, and the dogmatical elements of religion, which makes the contrast between the Prophets and all other sacred bodies which have existed in Pagan and, it must even be added, in Christian times. They were religious teachers without the usual faults of religious teachers: They were a religious body, whose only professional spirit was to be free from the usual prejudices, restraints, and crimes by which all other religious professions have been disfigured. They are not without grievous shortcomings; they are not on a level with the full light of the Christian

---

[r] St. Matt. xv. 1—20, xxiii.; St. Luke xv.   [s] Heb. x. 7.
[t] 2 Cor. iii. 6.   [u] 1 Cor. xiii. 1, 2.   [v] Ibid. xiv. 5.
[x] Rom. ii. 29; Gal. ii. 5, 20, vi. 15; Tit. ii. 8.
[y] 1 St. John ii. 3, 4; Jerom. ad Gal. vi.

Revelation. But, taken as a whole, the Prophetic order of the Jewish Church remains alone. It stands like one of those vast monuments of ancient days—with ramparts broken, with inscriptions defaced, but stretching from hill to hill, conveying in its long line of arches the rill of living water over deep valley and thirsty plain, far above all the puny modern buildings which have grown up at its feet, and into the midst of which it strides with its massive substructions, its gigantic height, its majestic proportions, unequalled and unrivalled.

<small>Example to the Christian Clergy.</small> We cannot attain to it. But even whilst we relinquish the hope—even whilst we admire the good Providence of God, which has preserved for us this unapproachable memorial of His purposes in former ages—there is still one calling in the world in which, if any, the Prophetic spirit, the Prophetic mission, ought at least in part to live on, and that is, the calling of the Christian clergy. We are not like the Jewish Priests, we are not like the Jewish Levites, but we have, God be praised, some faint resemblances to the Jewish Prophets. Like them, we are chosen from no single family or caste; like them, we are called not to merely ritual acts, but to teach and instruct; like them, we are brought up in great institutions[z] which pride themselves on fostering the spirit of the Church in the persons of its ministers. O glorious profession, if we would see ourselves in this our true Prophetic aspect! We all know what a powerful motive in the human

---

[z] Comp. 1 Sam. x. 10, xix. 20; 2 Kings ii. 3.

mind is the spirit of the order, the spirit of a profession, the *spirit* (as the French say) of the *body*, to which we belong. O if the spirit of our profession, of our order, of our body, were the spirit, or anything like the spirit, of the ancient Prophets! if with us truth, charity, justice, fairness to opponents, were a passion, a doctrine, a point of honour, to be upheld, through good report and evil, with the same energy as that with which we uphold our position, our opinions, our interpretations, our partnerships! A distinguished prelate [a] has well said, "It makes all the difference in the world whether "we put the duty of Truth in the first place, or in "the second place." Yes: that is exactly the difference between the spirit of the world and the spirit of the Bible. The spirit of the world asks, *first*, "Is it safe, Is it pious?" secondly, "Is it "true?" The spirit of the Prophets asks, *first*, "Is it true?" secondly, "Is it safe?" The spirit of the world asks, *first*, "Is it prudent?" secondly, "Is it right?" The spirit of the Prophets asks, *first*, "Is it right?" secondly, "Is it prudent?" It is not that they and we hold different doctrines on these matters, but that we hold them in different proportions. What they put first, we put second; what we put second, they put first. The religious energy which we reserve for objects of temporary and secondary importance, they reserved for objects of eternal and primary importance. When Ambrose closed the doors of the church of Milan against the

[a] Archbishop Whately.

blood-stained hands of the devout Theodosius, he acted in the spirit of a prophet. When Ken, in spite of his doctrine of the Divine right of Kings, rebuked Charles II. on his death-bed for his long-unrepented vices, those who stood by were justly reminded of the ancient Prophets. When Savonarola, at Florence, threw the whole energy of his religious zeal into burning indignation against the sins of the city, high and low, his sermons read more like Hebrew prophecies than modern homilies.

We speak sometimes with disdain of moral essays, as dull, and dry, and lifeless. Dull, and dry, and lifeless they truly are, till the Prophetic spirit breathes into them. But let religious faith and love once find its chief, its proper vent in them, as it did of old in the Jewish Church—let a second Wesley arise who shall do what the Primate of his day wisely but vainly urged as his gravest [b] counsel on the first Wesley, that is, throw all the ardour of a Wesley into the great unmistakeable doctrines and duties of life as they are laid down by the Prophets of old and by Christ in the Gospels,—let *these* be preached with the same fervour as that with which Andrew Melville enforced Presbyterianism, or Laud enforced Episcopacy, or Whitfield enforced Assurance, or Calvin Predestination,—then, perchance, we shall understand in some degree what was the propelling energy of the Prophetic order in the Church and Commonwealth of Israel.

[b] See Wesley's Life, i. 222.

(3.) This is the most precious, the most supernatural, of all the Prophetic gifts. Let me pass on to the next, which brings out the same characteristic in another and equally peculiar aspect. The Prophets not merely laid down these general principles of theology and practice, but were the direct oracles and counsellors of their countrymen in action; and for this was required the Prophetic insight into the human heart, which enabled them to address themselves not merely to general circumstances, but to the special emergencies of each particular case. Often they were consulted even on trifling matters, or on stated occasions. So Saul wished to ask Samuel after his father: "When "men went to inquire of God, then they spake, "Come, let us go to the Seer^c." So the Shunamite went at new moons^d or Sabbaths, to consult the man of God on Carmel. But more usually they addressed themselves spontaneously to the persons or the circumstances which most needed encouragement or warning. Suddenly, whenever their interference was called for, they appeared, to encourage or to threaten; Elijah, before Ahab, like the ghost of the murdered Naboth on the vineyard of Jezreel; Isaiah, before Ahaz at the Fuller's Gate, before Hezekiah, as he lay panic-struck in the palace; Jeremiah, before Zedekiah; John, before Herod; the Greatest of all, before the Pharisees in the Temple. Whatever public or private calamity had occurred, was seized by them to move the national

Appeal to the consciences of the hearers.

1 Sam. ix. 9.   ^d 1 Kings iv. 23.

or individual conscience. Thus Elijah spoke, on occasion of the drought; Joel, on occasion of the swarm of locusts; Amos, on occasion of the earthquake. Thus, in the highest degree, our Lord, as has been often observed, drew His parables from the scenes immediately around Him. What the ear received slowly, was assisted by the eye. What the abstract doctrine failed to effect, was produced by its impersonation in the living forms of nature, in the domestic incidents of human intercourse. The Apostles, in this respect, by adopting the written mode of communication, are somewhat more removed from personal contact with those whom they taught than were the older Prophets. But St. Paul makes his personal presence so felt in all that he writes, fastens all his remarks so closely on existing circumstances, as to render his Epistles a means, as it were, of reproducing himself. He almost always conceives himself "present with them "in spirit [e]," as speaking to his reader "face to "face [f]." Every sentence is full of himself, of his readers, of his circumstances, of theirs. And in accordance with this is his description of the effect of Christian prophesying. "If all prophesy, and "there come in one that believeth not, or one "unlearned, he is convinced of all, he is judged of "all [g]." That is, one prophet after another shall take up the strain, and each shall reveal to him some fault which he knew not before. One after another shall ask questions which shall reveal to

[e] 1 Cor. v.   [f] 2 Cor. xiii. 2.   [g] 1 Cor. xiv. 24, 25.

him his inmost self, and sit as judge on his inmost thoughts, "and thus," the Apostle continues, "the "*secrets* of his *heart* are made *manifest*, and so falling "down on his face" (awe-struck), "he will worship "God, and report that God is *in you of a truth.*"

This is the true definition, by one of the mightiest Prophets, of what true Prophesying is—what it is in its effects, and why it is an evidence of a Real or Divine Presence wherever it is found. It is this close connexion with the thoughts of men—this appeal to their hearts and consciences—this reasoning together with every one of us, which, on the one hand, makes the interpretation of Scripture, especially of the Prophetic Scriptures, so dependent on our knowledge of the characters of those to whom each part is addressed; which, on the other hand, makes each portion bear its own lesson to each individual soul.—"Thou art the man[h]." So in the fulness of the Prophetic spirit Nathan spoke to David, and so in a hundred voices God through that goodly company of Prophets still speaks to us, and "convinces us" of our sin and of His Presence.

And has this Prophetic gift altogether passed away from our reach? Not altogether. That divine intuition, that sudden insight into the hearts of men, is indeed no longer ours, or ours only in a very limited sense. Still it fixes for us the standard at which all preachers and teachers should aim. Not our thoughts, but the thoughts of our hearers,

[h] 1 Sam. xii. 1.

is what we have to explain to ourselves and to them. Not in *our* language, but in theirs, must we speak if we mean to make ourselves understood by them. By talking with the humblest of the poor in the parishes where our lot as pastors will be cast, we shall gain the best materials—materials how rich and how varied and how just!—for our future sermons. By addressing ourselves, not to any imaginary congregation, or to any abstract and distant circumstances, but to the actual needs which we know, in the hearts of our neighbours and ourselves, we shall rouse the sleeper, and startle the sluggard, and convince the unbelievers, and enlighten the unlearned. So the great Athenian teacher,—the nearest approach to a Jewish or Christian Prophet that the Gentile world ever produced,—so Socrates worked his way into the minds of the Grecian, and so of the European world. "To "him," as has been well said by his modern biographer[1], "the prompt *Know thyself* was the holiest "of texts." He applied it to himself, he applied it to others, and the result was the birth of all philosophy. But not less is it the basis of all true prophesying, of all good preaching, of all sound preparation for the pastoral office.

Relations to their Country.

(4.) Another characteristic of the teaching of the Prophets to be briefly touched upon is to be found in their relation not to individuals, but to the State. At one time they were actually the leaders of the nation, as in the case of Moses, Deborah, Samuel,

[1] Grote's History of Greece, viii. 602.

David; in earlier times their function in this respect was chiefly to maintain the national spirit by appeals to the Divine help, and to the past recollections of their history. This function became more complex as the Israelitish affairs became more entangled with those of other nations. But still, throughout, three salient points stand out. The first is that, universal as their doctrine was, and far above any local restraints as it soared, they were thoroughly absorbed in devotion to their country. To say that they were patriots, that they were good citizens, is a very imperfect representation of this side of the Prophetic character. They were *one* with it, they were representatives of it; they mourned, they rejoiced with it, and for it, and through it. Often we cannot distinguish between the Prophet and the people for whom he speaks[k]. Of that uneasy hostility to the national mind, which has sometimes marked even the noblest of disappointed politicians and of disaffected Churchmen, there is hardly any trace in the Hebrew Prophet. And although with the changed relations of the Jewish Commonwealth, the New Testament Prophets could no longer hold the same position, yet even then the national feeling is not extinct. Christ Himself wept over His country[l]. His Prophecy over Jerusalem[m] is a direct continuation of the strain of the older Prophets. The same may be said of St. Paul's passionate allusions to his love for the Jewish people in the Epistle

Patriotism.

---

[k] See especially Isa. xl.—liv.; Lamentations iii. 1—66.
[l] St. Luke xix. 41.   [m] St. Matt. xxiv.

to the Romans[n], which are almost identical with those of Moses[o]. I will not go further into the enlargement of this feeling, as it followed the expansion of the Jewish into the Christian Church. It is enough that our attention should be called to this example for the teachers of every age. Public spirit, devotion to a public cause, indignation at a public wrong, enthusiasm in the national welfare, —this was not below the loftiest of the ancient Prophets; it surely is still within the reach of the humblest of Christian teachers.

Again, they laboured to maintain, and did to a considerable degree maintain, in spite of the divergence of tribes and disruption of the monarchy, the state of national unity. The speech of Oded reproaching the northern kings for the sale of the prisoners of the south is a sample of the whole prophetic spirit. "Now ye purpose to keep under "the children of Judah and Jerusalem for bondmen "and bondwomen unto you: but are there not "with you, even with you, sins against the Lord "your God[p]?" To balance the faults of one part of the nation against the other in equal scales, was their difficult but constant duty[q]. To look forward to the time when Judah should no more vex Ephraim, nor Ephraim envy Judah[r], was one of their brightest hopes. If at times they increased the bitterness of the division, yet on the whole their aim was union, founded on a sense of their

Maintenance of National Unity.

[n] Rom. ix. 3, x. 1, xi. 1.   [o] Exod. xxxii. 32.
[p] 2 Chron. xxviii. 10.   [q] Ezek. xvi.   [r] Isa. xi. 13.

common origin and worship, overpowering the sense of their separation and alienation.

And thirdly, and as a consequence of this, we are struck by the variety, the moderation of the Prophetical teaching, changing with the events of their time.

It is instructive to see how at different epochs different evils attracted their attention; how the same institutions, which at one time seemed good, at another seemed fraught with evil. Contrast Isaiah's denunciation of the hierarchy with Malachi's support of them[s]. Contrast Isaiah's confidence against Assyria with Jeremiah's despair before Chaldæa[t]. There is no one Shibboleth handed through the whole series. Only the simple faith in a few great moral and religious principles remain, the rest is constantly changing. Only the poor are constantly protected against the rich; only the weaker side is always regarded with the tender compassion which belongs especially to Him to whom all the Prophets bare witness. To the poor, to the oppressed, to the neglected, the Prophet of old was and is still the faithful friend[u]. To the selfish, the luxurious, the insolent, the idle, the frivolous, the Prophet was and is still an implacable enemy.

Simplicity of principle and variety of application.

---

[s] Isa. i. 10; Malachi i. 8. (See Arnold's Life, i. 259.)
[t] Isa. xxxvii. 6; Jer. xxxvii. 8.
[u] Isa. iii. 14, v. 8, xxxii. 5; Jer. v. 5, xxii. 13; Amos vi. 3; St. James v. 1. (See Arnold's Letters on this subject. Nov. 1830. Life and Corresp., i. 234, 235.)

It is this aspect which has most forcibly brought out the well-known likeness of the Prophets both to ancient orators and modern statesmen[x]. The often quoted lines of Milton[y] best express both the resemblance and the difference:—

> " Their orators thou then extoll'st, as those
> The top of eloquence; statists indeed,
> And lovers of their country, as may seem;
> But herein to our Prophets far beneath,
> As men divinely taught, and better teaching
> The solid rules of civil government,
> In their majestic, unaffected style,
> Than all the oratory of Greece and Rome.
> In them is plainest taught, and easiest learnt,
> What makes a nation happy, and keeps it so,
> What ruins kingdoms, and lays cities flat;
> Those only with our law best form a king[y]."

Independence. (5.) One point yet remains in connexion with their teaching—and that is their absolute independence. Most of them were in opposition to the prevailing opinion of their countrymen for the time being. Some of them were persecuted, some of them were in favour with God and man alike. But in all, there was the same Divine Prophetic spirit—of elevation above the passions, and prejudices, and distractions of common life. " Be not afraid of them " —be not afraid of their faces—be not afraid of " their words. Speak My words unto them, whe-" ther they will hear, or whether they will for-

---

[x] Comp. Hebrew Politics in the Time of Sennacherib and Sargon, by Sir E. Strachey; also The Prophets of the Old Testament; Tracts for Priest and People, No. 8.
[y] Paradise Regained, iv. 353.

"bear." "I have made thy face strong against
"their faces, and thy forehead strong against their
"foreheads: as an adamant stronger than flint I
"have made thy forehead; fear them not, neither
"be dismayed[z]." This is the position of all the
Prophets, in a greater or less degree — it is the
position, in the very highest sense of all, of Him
whose chief outward characteristic it was that He
stood high above all the influences of His age, and
was the Rock against which they dashed in vain,
and on which they were ground to powder. This
element of the Prophetical Office deserves special
consideration, because it pervades their whole
teaching, and because it is in its lower manifestations within the reach of all. What is it that is
thus recommended to us? Not eccentricity, not
singularity, not useless opposition to the existing
framework of the world, or the Church in which
we find ourselves. Not this—which is of no use
to any one—but this which is needed by every one
of us, a fixed resolution to hold our own against
chance and accident, against popular clamour and
popular favour—against the opinions, the conversation, of the circle in which we live: a silent look
of disapproval, a single word of cheering approval
—an even course, which turns not to the right hand
or to the left, unless with our own full conviction—
a calm, cheerful, hopeful endeavour to do the work
that has been given us to do, whether we succeed
or whether we fail.

Ezek. ii. 6, 7, iii. 8, 9.

And for this Prophetic independence, what is, what was, the Prophetic ground and guarantee? There were two. One was that of which I will proceed to speak presently—that which has almost changed the meaning of the name of the Prophets—their constant looking forward to the Future. The other was that they felt themselves standing on a rock that was higher and stronger than they—the support and the presence of God. It was this which made their independent elevation itself a Prophecy, because it spoke of a Power behind them, unseen, yet manifesting itself through them in that one quality which even the world cannot fail at last to recognise. Give us a man, young or old, high or low, on whom we know that we can thoroughly depend,—who will stand firm when others fail,—the friend faithful and true, the adviser honest and fearless, the adversary just and chivalrous; in such an one there is a fragment of the Rock of Ages—a sign that there has been a Prophet amongst us.

The consciousness of the *presence of God.* In the Mussulman or the Hindoo this makes itself felt in the entire abstraction of the mind from all outward things. In the fanatic, of whatever religion, it makes itself felt in the disregard of all the common rules of human morality. In the Hebrew Prophet it makes itself felt in the indifference to human praise or blame, in the unswerving fidelity to the voice of duty and of conscience, in the courage to say what he knew to be true, and to do what he knew to be right. This in the Hebrew prophet—this in the Christian man—is the best sign of the near vision of Almighty God; it is the best sign of the Real Presence of Jesus Christ, the Faithful and True, the Holy and the Just, the Power of God, and the Wisdom of God.

III. This brings us to the Prophetic teaching of the Future. It is well known that in the popular and modern use of the word since the seventeenth century, by a "Prophet" is meant almost exclusively one who predicts or foretells; and to have asserted the contrary has even been thought heretical. It is evident that this assumption is itself a grave error[a]. It is wholly unauthorized, either by the Bible or by our own Church. It has drawn off the attention of the fundamental idea of the Prophetical office to a subordinate part. It has caused us to seek the evidence of Prophecy in those portions of it which are least convincing, rather than in those which are most convincing—in those parts which it has most in common with other systems, rather than in those parts which distinguish it from all other systems.

But this error, resting as it does on an etymological mistake, could never have obtained so wide

The Prophetic teaching of the Future.

---

[a] "It is simply a mistake to regard prediction as synonymous with prophecy, or even as the chief portion of a prophet's duties. Whether the language be Hebrew, Greek, or Latin, the ancient words for prophecy all refer to a state of mind, an emotion, an influence, and not to prescience."—Mr. Payne Smith's *Messianic Interpretation of Isaiah, Introd.*, p. xxx.

a diffusion, without some ground in fact; and this ground is to be found in the vast relation of the Prophetic office to the future, which I shall now attempt to draw forth—dwelling, as before, on the general spirit of the institution.

Prospective and predictive tendencies.

It is, then, undoubtedly true that the Prophets of the Old Dispensation did in a marked and especial manner look forward to the future. It was this which gave to the whole Jewish nation an upward, forward, progressive character, such as no Asiatic, no ancient, I may almost say, no other nation has ever had in the same degree. Representing as they did the whole people, they shared and they personated the general spirit of tenacious trust and hope that distinguishes the people itself. Their warnings, their consolations, their precepts, when relating to the past and the present, are clothed in imagery drawn from the future. The very form of the Hebrew verb, in which one tense is used for the past and for the future, lends itself to this mode of speech. They were conceived as shepherds[b] seated on the top of one of the hills of Judæa, seeing far over the heads of their flocks, and guiding them accordingly; or as watchmen standing on some lofty tower, with a wider horizon within their view than that of ordinary men. "Watchman, "what of the night? Watchman, what of the "night[c]?" was the question addressed to Isaiah by an anxious world below. "I will stand upon

[b] Isa. lvi. 10, 11. [c] Ibid. xxi. 11.

"my watch," is the expression of Habakkuk [d], "and set me upon the tower, and will watch to "see what He will say unto me. Though the "vision tarry, wait for it: it will surely come; it "will not tarry." Their practical and religious exhortations were, it is true, conveyed with a force which needed no further attestation. Of all of them, in a certain sense, it might be said as of the Greatest of all, that they spoke as one having authority and not as the scribes. Still there are special signs of authority besides, and of these, one of the chief, from first to last, was their "*speak-* "*ing things to come* [e]." And this token of Divinity extends (and here again I speak quite irrespectively of any special fulfilments of special predictions) to the whole Prophetic order, in Old and New Testament alike. There is nothing which to any reflecting mind is more signal a proof of the Bible being really the guiding book of the world's history, than its anticipations, predictions, insight into the wants of men far beyond the age in which it was written. That modern element which we find in it,—so like our own times, so unlike the ancient framework of its natural form—that Gentile, European, turn of thought,— so unlike the Asiatic

---

[d] Hab. ii. 1.

[e] It is observable that although the power of prediction is never made the test of a true prophet, (some of the greatest of them, Samuel, for example, Elijah and John the Baptist, having uttered either no prediction or only such as were very subordinate,) the failure of a prediction is in one remarkable passage made the test of a false prophet. Deut. xviii. 22.

language and scenery which was its cradle,—that enforcement of principles and duties, which for years and centuries lay almost unperceived, because hardly ever understood in its sacred pages; but which now we see to be in accordance with the utmost requirements of philosophy and civilization; those principles of toleration, chivalry, discrimination, proportion, which even now are not appreciated as they ought to be, and which only can be fully realized in ages yet to come; these are the unmistakeable predictions of the Prophetic spirit of the Bible, the pledges of its inexhaustible resources.

Thus much for the general aspect of the Prophetical office as it looked to the Future. Its more special aspects may be considered under three heads.

<small>Political predictions.</small> (1.) First, their contemplation and prediction of the political events of their own and the surrounding nations. It is this which brings them most nearly into comparison with the seers of other ages and other races. Every one knows instances, both in ancient and modern times, of predictions which have been uttered and fulfilled in regard to events of this kind. Sometimes such predictions have been the result of political foresight. "To have "made predictions which have been often verified "by the event, seldom or never falsified by it'," has been suggested by one well competent to judge, as an ordinary sign of statesmanship in modern

---

' Mill's Representative Government, 224.

times. "To see events in their beginnings, to "discern their purport and tendencies from the "first, to forewarn his countrymen accordingly," was the foremost duty of an ancient orator, as described by Demosthenes[g]. Many instances will occur to students of history. Even within our own memory the great catastrophe of the disruption of the United States of America was foretold, even with the exact date[h], several years beforehand. Sometimes there has been an anticipation of some future epoch in the pregnant sayings of eminent philosophers or poets; as for example, the intimation of the discovery of America by Seneca; or of Shakspeare by Plato, or the Reformation by Dante. Sometimes the same result has been produced by a power of divination granted, in some inexplicable manner, to ordinary men. Of such a kind were many of the ancient oracles, the fulfilment of which, according to Cicero[i], could not be denied without a perversion of all history. Such was the foreshadowing of the twelve centuries of Roman dominion by the legend of the apparition of the twelve vultures to Romulus[k], and which were so understood[l] four hundred years before its actual accomplishment. Such, but with less certainty, was the traditional prediction of the conquest of Constantinople by the Mussulmans; the alleged predic-

[g] De Corona, 73. See Sir E. Strachey on the Prophets of the Old Testament, pp. 2, 29.
[h] Spence on the American Union, p. 7.   [i] Cic., De Divinatione, i. 19.   [k] Gibbon, c. 35.   [l] Ibid., c. 52.

tions[m] by Archbishop Malachi, whether composed in the eleventh or the sixteenth century, of the series of Popes down to the present time; not to speak of the well-known instances which are recorded both in French and English history. But there are several points which at once place the Prophetic predictions on a different level from any of these. It is not that they are more exact in particulars of time and place; none can be more so than that of the twelve centuries of the Roman Empire; and our Lord Himself has excluded the precise knowledge of times and seasons from the widest and highest range of the prophetic vision. The difference rather lies in their close connection with the moral and spiritual character of the Prophetic mission, and their freedom (for the most part) from any of those fantastic and arbitrary accompaniments by which so many secular predictions are distinguished. They are almost always founded on the denunciations of moral evil, or the exaltation of moral good, not on the mere localities or cities concerned. The nations whose doom is pronounced thus become representatives of moral principles and examples to all ages alike. Israel, Jerusalem, Egypt, Babylon, Tyre[n], are personifications of states or

[m] For this, and many other instances of more or less value, see a collection in Das Buch der Wahr- und Weis-Sagungen, published at Ratisbon, 1850, or in an abridged form in French, Le Livre de Toutes les Prophéties et Prédictions, Paris, 1849.

[n] This is well brought out in Arnold's Sermons on Prophecy.

principles still existing, and thus the predictions concerning them have, as Lord Bacon says, constantly germinant fulfilments. The secular events which are thus predicted, are (with a few possible exceptions[o]) within the horizon of the Prophet's age, and are thus capable of being turned to the practical edification of the Prophet's own age and country. As in the vision of Pisgah, the background is suggested by the foreground. No object is introduced which a contemporary could fail to appreciate and understand in outline, although its remoter and fuller meaning might be reserved for a far distant future. These predictions are also, in several striking instances, made dependent on the moral condition of those to whom they are addressed, and are thus divested of the appearance of blind caprice or arbitrary fate, in which the literal predictions of both ancient and modern divination so much delight. " Yet forty days and " Nineveh shall be overthrown." No denunciation is more absolute in its terms than this; and of none is the frustration more complete. The true Prophetic lesson of the Book of Jonah is, that there was a principle in the moral government of God, more sacred and more peremptory even than the accomplishment of the most cherished prediction. " God saw their works, that they turned from their

---

[o] The cases referred to are such as need not be here discussed. They are either confessedly exceptional, or else admit (on quite independent grounds) of another explanation; and they can only be treated justly by being considered in detail.

"evil way; and God repented of the evil, that
"He had said that He would do unto them; and
"He did it not[p]." What here appears in a single
case is laid down as a universal rule by the Prophet
Jeremiah. "At what instant I shall speak con-
"cerning a nation . . . to destroy it; if that na-
"tion . . . turn from their evil, I will repent of the
"evil that I thought to do unto them. And at
"what instant I shall speak concerning a nation
". . . to build and to plant it; if it do evil in My
"sight, that it obey not My voice, then I will re-
"pent of the good wherewith I said I would benefit
"them[q]."

With these limitations, it is acknowledged by
all students of the subject, that the Hebrew Prophets made predictions concerning the fortunes of
their own and other countries which were un-
questionably fulfilled[r]. There can be no reasonable
doubt, for example, that Amos foretold the captivity and return of Israel; and Micah the fall of
Samaria; and Ezekiel the fall of Jerusalem; and
Isaiah the fall of Tyre; and Jeremiah the limits of
the Captivity. But, even if no such special cases
could be proved, the grandeur of the position which
the Prophets occupy in this respect is one which
it needs no attestation of any particular prediction
to enhance, and which no failure of any particular
prediction can impair. From those lofty watch-
towers of Divine speculation, from that moral and

[p] Jonah iii. 10.   [q] Jer. xviii. 7—9.
[r] See Ewald, Geschichte des Volkes Israel, iii. 303.

spiritual height which raised them far above the rest of the ancient world, they saw the rise and fall of other nations, long before it was visible to those nations themselves. "They were the first in all "antiquity," it has been well said[s], "to perceive "that the old East was dead; they celebrated its "obsequies, in advance of the dissolution which "they saw to be inevitable." They were, as Dean Milman[t] has finely expressed it, the "great Tragic "Chorus of the awful drama that was unfolding "itself in the Eastern world. As each independ- "ent tribe or monarchy was swallowed up in the "universal empire of Assyria, the seers of Judah "watched the progress of the invader, and uttered "their sublime funeral anthems over the greatness "and prosperity of Moab and Ammon, Damascus "and Tyre." And in those funeral laments and wide-reaching predictions we trace a foretaste of that universal sympathy with nations outside the chosen circle,—of that belief in an all-embracing Providence,—which has now become part of the belief of the highest intelligence of the world. There may be many innocent questions about the date, or about the interpretation of the Book of Daniel, and of the Apocalypse. But there can be no doubt that they contain the first germs of the great idea of the succession of ages, of the continuous growth of empires and races under a law of Divine Providence, the first sketch of the Education

[s] Quinet, Génie des Religions, p. 372.
[t] History of the Jews, i. 298.

of the world, and the first outline of the Philosophy of History[u].

Messianic Predictions.

(2.) I pass to the second grand example of the predictive spirit of the Prophets. It was the distinguishing mark of the Jewish people that their golden age was not in the past, but in the future; that their greatest Hero (as they deemed Him to be) was not their founder, but their founder's latest descendant. Their traditions, their fancies, their glories, gathered round the head not of a chief, or warrior, or sage that had been, but of a King, a Deliverer, a Prophet who was to come. Of this singular expectation the Prophets were, if not the chief authors, at least the chief exponents. Sometimes He is named, sometimes He is unnamed; sometimes He is almost identified with some actual Prince of the coming or the present generation; sometimes He recedes into the distant ages[x]. But again and again, at least in the later Prophetic writings, the vista is closed by His person, His character, His reign. And almost everywhere the Prophetic spirit, in the delineation of His coming, remains true to itself. He is to be a King, a Conqueror, yet not by the common weapons of earthly warfare, but by those only weapons which the Prophetic order recognised—by justice[y], mercy, truth, and goodness,—by suffering, by endurance, by iden-

---

[u] See Lücke on St. John, iv. 156.

[x] See Ewald, iii. 360—363.

[y] Ps. xlv. 4, lxxii. 11—14; Isa. xl. 1—9, liii. 1—9; Jer. xxiii. 5, 6.

tification of Himself with the joys, the sufferings of His nation, by opening a wider sympathy to the whole human race than had ever been opened before. That this expectation, however explained, existed in a greater or less degree amongst the Prophets, is not doubted by any theologians of any school whatever. It is no matter of controversy. It is a simple and universally recognised fact,— that, filled with these Prophetic images, the whole Jewish nation — nay, at last the whole Eastern world—did look forward with longing expectation to the coming of this future Conqueror. Was this unparalleled expectation realized? And here again I speak only of facts which are acknowledged by Germans and Frenchmen, no less than by Englishmen, by critics and by sceptics, even more fully than by theologians and ecclesiastics. There did arise out of this nation a Character by universal consent as unparalleled as the expectation which had preceded Him. Jesus of Nazareth was, on the most superficial no less than on the deepest view we take of His coming, the greatest name, the most extraordinary power, that has ever crossed the stage of History. And this greatness consisted not in outward power, but precisely in those qualities in which from first to last the Prophetic order had laid the utmost stress—justice and love, goodness and truth.

I push this argument no further. Its force is weakened the moment we introduce into it any controverted detail. The fact which arrests our attention is, that side by side with this great expectation, appears the great climax to which the whole History leads up. It is a proof, if anything can be a proof, of a unity of design in the education of the Jews, in the history of the world. It is a proof that the events of the Christian Dispensation were planted on the very centre of human hopes and fears. It is a proof that the noblest hopes and aspirations that were ever breathed, were not disappointed; and that when "God spake by the Prophets" of the coming Christ, He spake of that which in His own good time He was certain to bring to pass.

(3.) There is one further class of predictions in which the Prophetic writings abound, and which still more directly connects itself with their general spirit, and of which the predictions I have already noticed are only a part—the Future, as a ground of consolation to the Church, to individuals, to the human race. It is this which gives to the Bible at large that hopeful, victorious, triumphant character, which distinguishes it from the morose, querulous, narrow, desponding spirit of so much false religion, ancient and modern. *The Power of the Future.*— This is the fulcrum by which they kept up the hopes of their country, and on its support we can rest as well as they.

<small>Predictions of the Church.</small>

The Future of the Church.—I need not repeat those glorious predictions which are familiar to all. But their spirit is applicable now as well as then. Although, in this sense, we prophesy and predict, as it were, at second-hand from them, yet our anticipations are so much the more certain, as they are justified and confirmed by the experience, which the Prophets had not, of two thousand years ago. We may be depressed by this or that failure of good projects, of lofty aspirations. But the Prophets and the Bible bid us look onward. The world, they tell us, as a whole tends forwards and not backwards. The losses and backslidings of this generation, if so be, will be repaired in the advance of the next. " To one far off Divine event," slowly it may be and uncertainly, but still steadily onwards, " the " whole creation moves." Work on in faith, in hope, in confidence; the future of the Church, the future of each particular society in which our lot is cast, is a solid basis of cheerful perseverance. The very ignorance of the true spirit of the Bible of which we complain, is the best pledge of its boundless resources for the future. The doctrines, the precepts, the institutions, which as yet lie undeveloped, far exceed in richness, in power, those that have been used out or been fully applied.

The Future of the Individual.—Have we ever thought of the immense stress laid by the Prophets on this mighty thought? What is the sentence with which the Church of England opens its morning and evening service, but a Prophecy, a Prediction, of the utmost importance to every human soul? "When the wicked man shall turn away "from his wickedness, and doeth that which is law- "ful and right, *he shall save his soul alive.*" So

<small>Predictions of the Individual</small>

spoke Ezekiel[a], advancing beyond the limits of the Mosaic law. So spoke no less Isaiah and Micah: "Though your sins be as scarlet, they shall be as "white as snow[a]." "He will turn again; He will "have compassion upon us. He will subdue our "iniquities. Thou wilt cast all their sins into the "depths of the sea[b]." So spoke, in still more endearing accents, the Prophet of Prophets, Jesus Christ Himself, when He uttered His world-wide invitation, "Him that cometh to Me, I will in "no wise cast out." "Her sins which are many "are forgiven." "Go and sin no more." The Future is everything to us, the Past is nothing. The turn, the change, the fixing our faces in the right, instead of the wrong direction—this is the difficulty—this is the turning-point—this is the crisis of life. But that once done, the Future is clear before us. The despondency of the human heart, the timidity or the austerity of Churches or of sects, may refuse this great Prophetic absolution; may cling to penances and regrets for the past; may shrink from the glad tidings that the good deeds of the Future can blot out the sorrows and the sins of the Past. But the whole Prophetic teaching of the Old and New Testament has staked itself on the issue; it hazards the bold prediction that all will be well when once we have turned; it bids us go courageously forward, in the strength of the Spirit of God, in the power of the life of Christ.

[z] Ezek. xviii. 27.   [a] Isa. i. 18.   [b] Micah vii. 19.

There is yet one more Future,—a *future* which to the Prophets of old was almost shut out, but which it is the glory of the Prophets of the New Dispensation to have predicted to us with unshaken certainty,—the Future life. In this respect, the predictions of the latest of the Prophets far transcend those which went before. The heathen philosophers were content with guesses on the immortal future of the soul. The elder Hebrew Prophets were content, for the most part, with the consciousness of the Divine support in this life and through the terrors of death, but did not venture to look further. But the Christian Prophets, gathering up the last hopes of the Jewish Church into the first hopes of the Christian Church, throw themselves boldly on the undiscovered world beyond the grave, and foretell that there the wishes and fears of this world would find their true accomplishment. To this Prediction so confident, yet so strange at the time, the intelligence no less than the devotion of mankind has in the course of ages come round. Powerful minds, which have rejected much beside in the teaching of the Bible, have claimed as their own this last expectation of the simple Prophetic school, which founded its hopes on the events of that first Easter-day, that first day of the week, "when life and immortality were brought to light." And it is a prediction which shares the character of all the other truly Prophetic utterances; in that it directly bears on the present state of being. Even without dwelling on the special doctrine of judgment and retribution, the mere fact of the stress laid by the Prophets on the certainty of the Future is full of instruction, hardly perhaps enough borne in mind. Look forwards, we sometimes say, a few days or a few months, and how differently will all things seem. Yes: but look forwards a few more years, and how yet more differently will all things seem. From the height of that Future, to which on the wings of the ancient Prophetic belief we can transport ourselves, look back on the present. Think of our pleasures, as they will seem to us then. Think of our troubles, as they will seem when we know their end. Think of those good thoughts and deeds which alone will survive in that unknown world. Think of our controversies, as they will appear, when we shall be forced to sit down at the feast with those whom we have known only as opponents here, but whom we must recognise as companions there. To that Future of Futures which shall fulfil the yearnings of all that the Prophets have desired on earth, it is for us, wherever we are, to look onwards, upwards, and forwards, through Jesus Christ, the same yesterday and for ever.

SERMON III.

God hath spoken by His Son.

PREACHED IN CHRIST CHURCH CATHEDRAL,

ON THE NINETEENTH SUNDAY AFTER TRINITY,

OCTOBER 26, 1862.

SERMON III.

HEBREWS i. 1, 2.

God . . . . hath in these last days spoken unto us by His Son.

THIS is the concluding portion of that great text —that fullest definition that the Bible contains of its own Revelation—on which I have twice before addressed you. In my first Sermon, I pointed out the " sundry times and divers manners," the gradual, partial, progressive character of the whole Revelation. In my second, I dwelt on the special point on which the Revelation of the Old Testament was concentrated, namely, " God spake by the Pro-" phets." In this, my last and concluding Sermon, I have to dwell on the special point on which the Revelation of the New Testament is concentrated. " God hath in these last days spoken to " us ' in' His Son."

I have often dwelt on the necessity of preserving the due proportion of faith. Almost all heresies, extravagancies, and eccentricities in religion, have (as the very words imply) arisen from their wandering outside the orbit, away from the centre to some narrow or insignificant point of their own choice or fancy, which, neglectful of the essential features of the world, the Church, and the Bible, has been pushed into undue celebrity and importance. The task of rightly selecting the chief doctrine of our faith or of our theology is like the selection of the site for a capital city. You have seen, it may be, a vast plain, with a noble river, on the banks of which a splendid city might have grown and spread, and sent forth its merchandize and its armies; and you see instead, that it has, from some caprice of its founder, been planted on a corner of a small stream, where it cannot expand, and where its growth is destructive to its health, its beauty, its usefulness. Or you may have seen it fixed, by another caprice, in the centre of a country, without water, without verdure, without hills; the nominal centre, but with nothing central except the name; a drain, an incubus on the national life, and not its heart or its head. Such have been many of the capital doctrines of later theological systems; true or half true in themselves, but deprived of their own vitality, and depriving other truths of their vitality, by assuming a prominence for which they had no natural fitness.

But such was not the proportion of doctrine either in the Bible or in the ancient Church.

The Revelation of Christ the central doctrine of the Bible. The central doctrine of the New Testament was—indeed it could hardly be otherwise—that which is briefly expressed in the text, "God spoke by His Son." He spoke, no doubt, by the Prophets of old: this I set forth when last I spoke to you. But put the Prophets, put the Hebrew Scriptures, as high as we will, they are not the last, they are not the clearest, they are not the most perfect, expressions of the Divine will. To me indeed, (if I may speak for a moment of myself,) the history of the Jewish Church has an interest so intense, a value so enormous, that I could fain adopt any expression, however fervent, of veneration for the ancient Scriptures which contain it. But this veneration ought not to blind us to the fact that the Old Testament is not, and cannot be, equal to the New. " God spake by His Son" in a sense far more divine than even by Moses, or David, or Isaiah. To attack the New Testament through the sides of the Old, or to defend the Old Testament by making the New Testament identical with it, are courses not only unwarrantable in themselves, but directly contrary to the repeated declarations of the Bible, that there is a paramount and unapproachable superiority in the Revelation of God in Jesus Christ, above every other that He has ever vouchsafed to man.

And not only is this important in the comparison of the whole Christian dispensation with that of the ancient covenant; it is also important in adjusting the value of the different parts of the Christian Revelation with each other. Here again I may confidently re-assert the delight, which none can feel more strongly than I do, in the history of the Apostolic Age, and in the Epistles of the great Apostle of the Gentiles. But even these, by the same unerring test, are not the culminating points of the Christian Revelation. We are not told that " God " in these last days spoke to us" by Paul or Cephas, or even John—not even by Apostles or by Apostolic Churches—but "by His Son." The Acts and the Epistles are the applications, the manifestations of the Gospel. But the "Gospel" itself, which controls and guides all the rest—"the "Gospel," which is fitly chosen as the very name of our religion, is contained, as the word itself implies, in the Four Gospels—the record of the life and teaching of Him who is not only the Founder of our Religion, but is our Religion itself. The Gospel of St. John, as it is the end in point of time, so it is the climax in point of importance of the whole written Word of God.

The Incarnation the central doctrine of the early Church.

As it is in the doctrines of the Bible, so it is, from another point of view, in the doctrines of the early Church. In later ages of the Church, different truths or forms of Christianity have assumed the place of cardinal interest. Predestination, the mode of Justification, the Sacrament of the Eucharist, the independence of the State or the independence of the clergy, the supremacy or the inspiration of the Bible—each of these in turn has been regarded as the article of a falling or a standing Church. But not one of these has taken that place, not one of them is even named, in the early Creeds. The one truth around which those Creeds all gather, is the Incarnation. It is so in the Apostles' Creed; it is so in the Nicene Creed; it is so, although not quite so exclusively, in the Athanasian Creed. Pay as much or as little attention as we will to the language in which that doctrine was couched, still all must acknowledge that it holds the chief place. The great moral doctrines of the Gospel are of course above every theological statement whatever. But to elevate any theological doctrine into equality or superiority to the doctrine of the Incarnation—to represent any of the doctrines just named, however important, as essential parts of the Creed of Christendom—is to run directly counter to the language of the first four General Councils, and to the whole genius of the Catholic Faith and the Catholic Church.

Such being the case, I proceed to ask, in all reverence, why this is so? What are the points which make it fitting and natural, and full of instruction, that the most perfect Revelation of God should be that which is contained in His Son Jesus Christ? I do not profess to exhaust this great subject. I do not profess to defend, or to establish the doctrine. I take it as it stands in the Bible and in the Creeds; and I ask you to consider the meaning of this striking and incontrovertible selection of the Incarnation, as the central truth of the Bible.

"*God has spoken in His Son.*" The final Revelation of God is in the Person and Character of Jesus Christ. This is the statement of the text. What is its paramount significance and importance? What are its relations to the rest of our Christian belief?

1. First, the study of the Person, the Mind of Christ, is thus by the very force of the terms, the foundation of all Christian "theology" properly so

The Character of Christ the Revelation of God.

called—that which tells of the nature of God. We want to know what is the voice of God. The Bible answers, " It is the voice of Christ." I am not going to re-open those questions of late debated amongst us with so much zeal, and so much ability on both sides, as to the possibility of the finite comprehending the Infinite. But put the question as we like, it is certain that, on the one hand, we all of us, philosophers and simple men alike, have a vast difficulty in conceiving and analyzing the attributes and the nature of God. On the other hand, it is certain that, whatever answer philosophy may make to the question, the answer which the Bible makes is this : It states the difficulty as broadly as the most inveterate sceptic or dogmatist would desire : " No man hath seen God at any time." But it adds, " The only-begotten Son which is in the bosom of the Father, He hath declared Him." That is, in effect,—If we wish to know, if we are in perplexity to know, what are the essential characteristics of the Divine nature, look at the life and character of Christ. Whatever is the most vital part of His Character, is the most vital part of the Nature of God. By seeing, as we must see, that the most vital part is the moral character,—the Will, the Wisdom, the Love, the Justice, the Compassion, the Forbearance,—we learn beyond any matter of doubt, that these, according to the Bible, give the best conception we can form of the Divine Mind itself. These attributes of Christ carried to the highest pitch are, if the Bible and the Creeds speak true, of the very essence of Divinity. In adoring these, in adoring Him, we acknowledge that God is, above all other thoughts that we can have concerning Him, a moral Being. In this way it is that, according to the profound remark of a late lamented theologian, one grand result of the Nicene decision was the re-assertion of the Moral character, of the Moral perfection, of the Divine Nature. By these Christ-like, and therefore God-like qualities, by these if by any means whatever, we, weak and erring as we are, far more than by power, or wisdom, or costly offerings, or splendid rites, or correct belief, are enabled to hold communion with the Father of Spirits, who thus alone by us can be imagined or approached. In this way we are allowed to see that He is not a mere abstraction or general law, but that He, even as we see Him in His Son, is One whom we can love, and who can love and has loved us, even as we can love Christ, and as Christ has loved us. Christ is our Example. But He is much more than our Example. The whole spirit of His appearance is even more fully designed to shew us what God is, than to teach us what man ought to be. But we must not divide the two Natures; as though here we could trace a fragment of His Divinity, and there a fragment of His Humanity. The perfect Divinity is seen only through the perfect Humanity. He is one Christ, not two Christs. The more fearlessly we explore the depths of His example as the likeness of man, the more complete will be our knowledge of His revelation of the Mind of God[a]. It is one of the best of the dying

[a] "If our minds were but competent adequately to expand
"the idea included in that one word, GOD, we should need no-
"thing further, except consciousness of our own honest pur-
"pose, to set us at ease for time as well as eternity. But the
"Sacred Volume contains this expansion. In every part, but
"above all in the Four Gospels, it unfolds DEITY. It shews us
"Him, who dwelleth in the light which no man can approach
"unto, condescending to provide for the minutest of our wants,
"directing, guarding and assisting us, each hour and moment,
"with an infinitely more vigilant and exquisite care than our
"own utmost self-love can ever attain to. In order to perceive
"the glory and appreciate the excellence of our Redeemer, we
"must see Him in His own light and estimate Him by the
"standard He has Himself afforded. We must take His own
"account of the motives which engaged Him to assume our flesh
"and to tabernacle amongst us. In His Divine discourses He
"has made both His design and Himself known to us. We
"can be wise therefore only by receiving this instruction; and
"happy only by improving this acquaintance. In thus appeal-
"ing to our Redeemer Himself, it is far from my thought to
"question either the authority or the satisfactoriness of the
"apostolic doctrine. This also affords us invaluable instruction
"and infallible guidance. But it supposes, not supersedes, the
"immediate lessons of Incarnate GODHEAD. These have an in-
"communicable pre-eminence over all which was ever deliver-
"ed; inasmuch as to Him, who spoke, GOD gave not the Spirit,
"as He is intimated to give Himself in every other instance, by
"measure. Let us then, as we are most bounden, be ever
"mindful of what has been written for our learning, by the
"Apostles of our Lord and Saviour; but still, let it be our
"highest and holiest care to sit, as it were, with Mary at the
"feet of Him who spake as never man spake. Except we
"hearken to His gracious words, we cannot be certain that we
"are His disciples indeed; nor can we estimate what we lose,
"in so relying on the purest and highest streams as to draw
"less assiduously and less profoundly from the fountain."—
Remains of Alexander Knox, pp. 262, 335, 336; *quoted in*

speeches of a well-known French pastor,—" The "more Jesus Christ is God, the more is He man; "and the more He is man, the more is He God[b]." Paradoxical as this is in form, it is true in spirit. There is nothing in the Gospel history more divine than the Agony of Gethsemane or the Crucifixion on Calvary. In those depths of humiliation we can catch a likeness of the Divine glory which we miss even on the Mount of Transfiguration, or the Ascension from Olivet. In this sense the Incarnation is the last and crowning sanction of the first truth of the Bible, "In the image of God made "He man." It is the most complete declaration to the human race that in the mind and heart of man is the nearest approach that can be made to the nature of God. Whereas the Greek philosophers, it has been well said, included the Divinity in the knowledge of the natural world, it was reserved for the Christian revelation to shew, that though in a physical or metaphysical point of view God is all but inaccessible, He reveals Himself to us as a part of our knowledge of man; as in other parts of the Bible, so especially and chiefly in this grand truth of the Incarnation, that as man alone He is to be known, or is in any way comprehensible.

2. Into how many directions does this thought of the entire unity of God and Christ extend light *Dr. Ogilvie's Bampton Lectures*, p. 230. I have not dwelt on the Revelation of God in the *words* of Christ, because I have spoken at length on this subject elsewhere, in my Sermons on "The Unity of Evangelical and Apostolical Teaching."

The works of Christ the Revelation of God.

[b] Adolphe Monod's Farewells, p. 146.

and consolation! When we waver in our thoughts of what God is and of what He would have us do, what this or that event is intended to teach us, let us turn to the life of Christ. There we are intended to see—there we do see—what God wills for us, what He wishes for us, how He deals with us. The mighty works of Christ are, as He Himself tells us, not His own works, but the works of His Father:—" My Father worketh hitherto, " and I work."

And not merely the more general character of God, but even His more special attributes, appear in the character of Christ. "Full of Grace and " Truth." Many have been the feelings and acts in which men have believed that God would take pleasure; many are the feelings and acts in which He does take pleasure. But the two acts, the two states, which above all other states bring us near to Him, are those two which above all others were seen in the character of Christ—Grace, that is, love, sympathy, eagerness to shew favour, forgiveness, mercy; Truth, that is, truthfulness, sincerity, reality, justice. In Christ was the most gracious tenderness; in Christ was the most fearless truth. And what there was in Him, that we may be sure there must be in God, and in those in whom God delights.

These two were united in the character of Christ, and they were united in the work of Christ. In the work of His redemption, from first to last, these two qualities stand conspicuous. And as they are conspicuous in Him, so they are in God. In this great act it is most emphatically true that Christ and the Father are one. We may not confound the Persons, but neither may we divide the Substance. It may have been natural for our great Arian poet, in that striking but fantastic passage in the "Para-"dise Lost," by which so much of our popular theology is coloured, to represent the Father and the Son as in sharp conflict with each other, the one as the Source of stern justice, the other as the opposing Source of mercy and love. But such is not the doctrine of the Bible or of the Church. In the Sacrifice of Christ we see, if one may so say, the Sacrifice of God Himself. In the Love of Christ we see the Love of God; the Truth of God is shewn to us in the Truth of Christ. Christ forgives us because God forgives us; God forgives us because Christ forgives us. God, not apart from Christ, or against Christ, but "God *in Christ*[c] "has forgiven us;" "God *in Christ* was reconcil-"ing[d]" (such is the absolutely uniform language of Scripture) "the world to Himself:" not Himself to Himself, as if estranged from us, nor to the world, as though He hated us, but "the world to "Himself," as estranged by sin from Him. In that great Parable in which our Blessed Lord has set forth the mystery of redemption, it is the Father who draws near to meet the returning prodigal. Christ, in drawing all men near to Himself, draws them through Himself to the Father.

3. Thirdly, it is through the Character and

[c] Eph. iv. 32, ἐν Χριστῷ. [d] 2 Cor. v. 19.

<small>The character of Christ the explanation of His words and acts.</small>

the Person of Christ that all the facts and doctrines respecting Him receive their true meaning. "God speaks to us" not in any statement respecting His Son, however important, not in any work of His Son, however vast, but "*in His Son*" Himself. His words are great, His acts are great, but He Himself is greater than either. I will take two instances to explain my meaning,—His death and His resurrection. I take them, not for the sake (God forbid!) of reviving any of the disputes which have been raised concerning them, but in the humble hope that by recalling to our minds the true doctrine of the Bible and of the early Church, we may be able to join hands across the yawning rents which are now tending to divide one from the other those who are really agreed. There are many ways, no doubt, of approaching these subjects; but the best and simplest way is to approach them through the study of the character of Him who is Himself the Way, the Truth, and the Life. Most admirably has this been expressed in the famous allegory, where the Pilgrim casts off his burden at the foot of the Cross, and at the mouth of the Sepulchre:—

> "Blest Cross! blest Sepulchre! Blest rather be
> The Man that there was put to shame for me."

"Blest Cross." Yes,—blessed Death! blessed in its history, in its effects, in its consolations, in its warnings. "Blest Sepulchre." Yes,—blessed Grave! which by shewing the victory of Christ over death, brought life and immortality to light, and declared Him to be the Son of God with power. Blessed

Resurrection, the glory of Easter-day, the joy of the Christian Sunday, the hope of the Christian in life and in death.

But more blessed even than His Cross—more blessed even than His Resurrection—more blessed because it is that from which each of those great events and doctrines derive their force and meaning, is He Himself. Take away what we know of the character and life of Christ, and His crucifixion would become a mere exhibition of pain and suffering. It would be what it is in the religion of Mahomet, an execution but not a Sacrifice, because it would be without that Sacrifice of heart and will in which alone the God of Revelation has declared Himself to be well pleased. It is, as Anselm well observed, the Life and the Obedience which constitutes the merit of the Offering and the excellence of the Satisfaction. It is from the Life which culminated in the death that the Death derives its virtue. It is from the long Sacrifice of Nazareth and Capernaum that the one supreme Sacrifice on Calvary receives its living savour. It is by seeing the Eternal Spirit of His mind as He was before, that we are able to understand what He was then. It is not from the side of the Atonement that we should approach the Incarnation, but from the side of the Incarnation that we should approach the Atonement. It is not by any single act, but by all the acts of His life, from "His holy Nativity" up to "His glorious Ascension," that "our good Lord "has delivered us."

Of His death.

Of His Resurrection.

And not the less is this true of the Resurrection. Take it as a mere miracle or wonder, it is barren of results, it is difficult of proof, it is inferior to many wonders recorded in our own or in other religions. But take it as the close—the natural close, if one may so say—of the Life and Death which preceded it, and then, even whilst we may acknowledge its difficulties, we shall see its meaning; we shall see in it the pledge, not merely of one single Divine Immortality, not merely of the immortality of the human soul in general, but of the immortality of that which it most concerns us to know to be immortal, the eternal, victorious, undying strength of that Wisdom, Goodness, Truth, and boundless Love, which though despised and rejected of men, though crucified and dead and buried, could not be holden by the bands of death, but rose again to give to His Church and His religion that cheerful, triumphant, victorious hope, of itself the best proof and the best explanation of the Resurrection itself. "Christ is risen,"—so we thankfully repeat from the Bible. "God "of God, Light of Light, Very God of Very God,"—so we proudly repeat from the Creed. O my brethren, think of what these or like words meant in the mouths of the first Apostles! They could not divide their belief in Christ's Resurrection from their belief that we too must rise again to that divine life which had been manifested in Him. They could not divide their belief that He was the Son of God from their belief that they were bound to follow Him in life and in death as His devoted servants. The energy, the vitality, the courage of the early Christian Church was the living witness of the power and the truth of Christ's Resurrection. Our assurance, our unshaken confidence that the mind and spirit of Christ is identical with all that is most generous, most comprehensive, most free, most progressive, is at once the surest pledge of His divinity and the firmest support to those who are involved in the struggles of the present age; because we thus know that He who is our Lord and Master, has not been left behind us in the past, but has gone before us, and is still going before us in the Future.

4. This brings me to a further class of thoughts suggested by this subject. "God in these last days " spake by His Son." "In these last days:" the sacred writer describes the event as though there were something peculiarly appropriate in the revelation of God in Christ coming "at that edge and "verge of time," (so the words more exactly express it). We know that this was so then. But it is so still. "In these last days." On that edge and extremity of the ages, in which we stand in this generation, there is, it seems to me, an even greater force than when they were first uttered, in the words "God speaks to us in His Son." There are no doubt many voices of God in the world, many voices of God in the Bible, and "none of them," as the Apostle says, "is without signification." But, if there be any which can hope to make itself heard above the questionings and distractions of this

The Revelation of Christ in these last days.

tumultuous time, it is the voice of God in His Son —in the character and spirit of Jesus Christ. For, first, amidst all the shocks and changes of belief, this is the one part of our religion which not only has undergone least attack, but has actually grown in its hold on the understanding and affections of mankind. We are alarmed at the advance of negative theology, and the like. No one who has touched these questions at all can be free from anxiety. But it is precisely this stronghold of our faith that is declared even from those very quarters to be not only unassailed, but unassailable. I quote the words of no advocate of received opinions, of no English ecclesiastic, but of one whose name has become a byword for destructive criticism. "Is " it possible," he asks, " for the character of Christ " ever to be superseded? Is it possible to expect " a further and more perfect manifestation of re- " ligion, as we may expect a further and more " perfect manifestation of art, of science, or of " philosophy?" "No," he answers, with a clear- ness to which his critical turn of mind gives an almost unexampled emphasis,—"No, it is not " possible. The unity which existed in the mind " of Christ between the divine and human is such, " that never through all time can any religious " development rise above it, in spite of all the ad- " vances of art, science, or knowledge. And never " either, in our days or in the remotest future, " can any religious progress hope to rival the " gigantic step which humanity made through the "revolution effected by Christ. Never before or since has the unity of God and man been manifested in a character so supreme, in a power so creative, as thus to penetrate and transfigure a whole life, uniformly and without the slightest appreciable perturbation[e]." "As little as mankind will ever be without religion, so little will they ever be without Christ: an historical, not a mythical Christ; an individual, not a mere symbol. Christ remains to us: He remains to us as the highest we know and are capable of imagining within the sphere of religion; as He, without whose presence in the mind perfect piety is impossible. In Him we do still possess the sum and substance of the Christian faith[f]." These remarkable words, even if they do not concede,

[e] Strauss's Life of Christ, vol. ii. § 49, 3rd edit. It is remarkable that in Dr. Mill's well-known work on Pantheism, (p. 104,) he gives at length, as though it were Strauss's own sentiment, the objection that Christianity might possibly be represented by a new religion. It is this objection that Strauss proceeds to answer in the passage which I have cited in a somewhat condensed form, but which Dr. Mill has unfortunately given in such a disjointed form as to be hardly recognisable. I have ventured to notice (with all respect for so learned and excellent a divine) this misapprehension, as an instance of the oversights which can be induced even in a pious controversialist by the desire to make the opponent say that which it is supposed that he must say.

It may be that such a reference as is here made to the passage in question is open to misconstruction. But I am satisfied that to welcome unreservedly these indications of agreement wherever found is in strict conformity with the sound dictates of Christian charity and Christian wisdom.

[f] Strauss, Soliloquies, 67.

as yet surely they do, an immense vantage-ground, from which alone we might almost hope to win back the greater part of the outward history, which their author thought that he had wrested from us, are at least a testimony of the most undeniable kind to the power, the perpetuity, the divinity of that which after all is the keystone of the whole fabric.

And not only is this highest point of Christian fact and doctrine the one which presents the firmest front to inquiry and speculation, but it is also the one for which the thought of modern times has achieved the most, in the way of just appreciation and understanding. In the first four centuries there was no doubt as strong, perhaps a stronger, sense of the dogmatical or philosophic truth of our Lord's Divine Nature. In the middle ages there was as profound, perhaps a more profound devotion to His Person. In the period of the Reformation there may have been a deeper sense of thankfulness for His work of redemption. In the eighteenth century there may have been as strong a sense of the complete impersonation of human virtue in His acts and words. But I venture, without disparagement of previous ages, to express a humble yet firm conviction that never before our own age has there been so keen, so discriminating a perception of the peculiarities (if I may so speak), the essential, innermost, distinguishing marks of the unapproached and unapproachable Character described to us in the Four Gospels. We have not arrived at the end of it. Far from it.

In the very fact of the large traits of His life and character which still remain unexplored, lies a boundless hope for the future. But in the advances that have been made even within our own generation in apprehending new yet eternal characteristics of that Divine Mind, we may already feel a confident hope for the present. We may feel that, with all our shortcomings, we yet have been enabled, by penetrating deeper than heretofore into the recesses of the mind of Christ, to penetrate deeper into the presence of God.

Other ages dwelt exclusively on Bethlehem and on Calvary. It has been reserved for this age to fix its attention on the scenes which to ancient pilgrims had but little or no interest—the Mount of Olives and the Sea of Galilee; the scenes, not of a few hours or a few moments of our Blessed Lord's appearance, but of those long days and years which represent to us the whole Life, the whole manifestation of the Word made flesh and dwelling amongst us. O let us accept this slight yet joyful omen! O let us believe that in thus reaching down below the surface to the foundation, the corner-stone, of our religion, we have arrived, or we shall arrive, at something deeper and wider and truer than has ever been reached before—something which runs beneath and across the various divisions of Christendom — something which, because it was common ground and not peculiar, they have all hitherto suffered to go to neglect and decay, but which now, in these last days, O may

God grant that they may build up with all their united efforts till it overtops and outshines all besides!

The Revelation of Christ to us.

One final word of the text. "God in these last "days speaks by His Son *to us*." Already the author of that great Epistle was living in a generation which had not seen our Lord on earth; and we are further removed still. Yet still "to us," in every generation—to us in our generation, no less is this the one great message of God. The "Imitation "of Christ:" this is the one book of devotion which has won the affections of the whole of Christendom, because it is the one subject which is identical with Christianity itself. To be like Christ: this is the one object which the whole New Testament impresses upon us. He who is not like Christ, however correct his belief, is not a Christian except in name. He who is like Christ, amidst whatever differences, is a Christian indeed and in truth. To be one with Christ: this is a doctrine which we all shrink from stating, which we all shrink from hearing, because it appears to condemn us all alike. But we can at least "*follow*" Him; we can follow at a distance; we can set our faces in the direction to which His life and spirit point. When we speak of coming to Christ, of apprehending Christ, we can ask ourselves what those words mean; and we can remember that they mean an imitation of that Divine Character, which embraces not merely the commonplace virtues which are too vague or too universal to be applicable, but graces some of which, at least, are so definite and distinct, that we cannot mistake them. Constant exertion for the good of others; cheerfulness and unfailing courage; stedfast devotion to truth and to justice; to live in the world and yet above it; toleration even of those from whom there is the widest difference; an absolute fusion of religion and morality; an absolute repose on the justice and the love of God; a free and far-reaching acknowledgment of all the facts of the world and of human nature, combined with the loftiest ideal of heroic duty and of heavenly holiness — these are some of the unmistakeable landmarks of the character of Christ our Lord. If we cannot attain to them ourselves, we can at least admire them in others. If to be like Christ is too hard a task, let us at least try to be like them in whom we can recognise any or all of these graces. We have known such : we have seen in them these unearthly gifts, which raise them above the world whilst they are with us; which carry us with them to the other world when they are taken from us. To be like them is (in a measure) to be like Christ; to be with Christ hereafter is to be with them; and in that better world which now seems so very far away, we may humbly hope to be like Him, and like them, for we shall see Him as He is.

www.ingramcontent.com/pod-product-compliance
Lightning Source LLC
Chambersburg PA
CBHW022145160426
43197CB00009B/1430